St. Paul's Letter to the Celts

Bronwen Scott-Branagan

© 2014 by Bronwen J. Scott-Branagan

All rights reserved. No part of this book may be reproduced or transmitted in any form or by any means, electronic or mechanical, including photocopying, recording or by any information storage and retrieval system, without prior permission in writing from the publisher. The Copyright Act 1968 (the Act) allows a maximum of one chapter or 10% of the book, whichever is the greater, to be photocopied by any educational institution for its educational purposes provided that the educational institution (or body that administers it) has given a remuneration notice to Copyright Agency Limited (CAL) under the Act.

National Library of Australia
Cataloguing-in-Publication entry

Author: Scott-Branagan, Bronwen.

Title: St. Paul's Letter to the Celts/
B. J. Scott-Branagan.

ISBN:9780980282788 (paperback)

Subjects: Bible. Galatians--
Commentaries.Bible. Galatians--
Criticism, interpretation, etc.

Dewey Number:227.407

From the *ESV® Bible* (*The Holy Bible, English Standard Version®*), copyright 2001 by Crossway, a publishing ministry of Good News Publishers. Used by permission. All rights reserved.

TABLE OF CONTENTS

1. St. Paul's Letter to the Celts	5
2. Paul's Greeting, Part I: Chapter1.1-4	15
3. Paul's Greeting, Part II: Chapter 1. 3-5	23
4. Paul's Reason for Writing: Chapter 1. 6-9	31
5. Paul's Story: Chapter 1. 10-16	41
6. Paul's Retreat and Preparation: Ch. 1.17-24	51
7. Paul's Acceptance: Chapter 2. 1-10	57
8. Paul Condemned Hypocrisy: Ch. 2. 11-14	65
9. The Law or Faith: Chapter 2. 15-21	70
10. The Holy Spirit: The Way to Salvation: Ch. 3. 1-5	77
11. Abraham, Forebear of Jew and Gentile: Ch. 3. 6-9	83
12. Live by Faith or Be Cursed: Ch. 3. 10-14	89
13. The Law and the Promise to Abraham:.3.15-18	97
14. The Purpose of the Law: Ch. 3. 19-24	103
15. Justified Through Faith: Ch. 3.25-29	111
16. God's Family and the Backsliding Celts: 4.1-5	117
17. The Significance of Paul's Ailment: Ch. 4. 10-15	125
18. Spiritual Growth: Chapter 4. 16-20	131
19. Hagar and Sarah as Allegory: Ch. 4. 21-3	139
20. Christ Has Set Us Free: Chapter 5. 1- 6	147
21. Spiritual Health: Chapter 5. 7-1	155
22. Led by the Spirit: Chapter 5. 16-18	165
23. The Works of the Flesh -1: Ch. 5. 19-20a	169
24 The Works of the Flesh -2: Ch. 5. 20b-21	177
25. The Fruit of the Spirit -1: Ch. 5. 22a	185
26. The Fruit of the Spirit -2: Ch. 5. 22b-23	193
27. Guided by the Spirit: Ch. 5. 24-26	199
28. The New Life of the Christian: Ch. 6. 1-6	205
29. The New Life of Caring: Ch. 6. 7-10	211
30. Summary and Benediction: Ch. 6. 11-18	217
31. Concluding Remarks	223
Appendix I: A Brief Timeline of the Galatian Celts	226
Appendix II: Galatian Language	237
Appendix III: Galatian Religion	238
Appendix IV: Galatian Culture	239

Grace to you and peace

from

God our Father

and

the Lord Jesus Christ.
Galatians 1.3

≈1≈

ST. PAUL'S LETTER TO THE CELTS

What letter did Paul write to the Celts? It was *The Epistle of Paul the Apostle to the Galatians*, or *The Letter of Paul to the Gauls*. The Gauls were Celtic peoples whose history began back in the Iron Age. Over long centuries the tribes spread across most of central Europe and into Asia Minor.

By the time that Paul wrote his letter some of these Celtic tribes had been settled in part of what we now know as Turkey and as they were Gauls, it was known as Galatia. Although Paul directed his letter to the Galatian Christians, it continues to speak to all Celts, and indeed to all people, even today. It addressed specific issues that were particular problems that appeared unexpectedly at that time, but the underlying message to us is timeless.

In this introduction, we look briefly at the history of the Celts, the life of St. Paul, the reason he wrote the letter and the language he chose to use.

THE CELTS
The history of the Celts goes back to well before written records began. The tribes were nomadic and wandered over much of Europe and Asia Minor. Later it was recorded that the Gauls were blue-eyed, tall, war-like and were often known as Barbarians. The Gallish languages they spoke are now known as Continental Celtic. Over time, as they arrived in suitable places, some of the groups settled and made more permanent homes.[1]

---

[1] Refer to the Appendices on pages 203 – 216 for more information about the history of the Galatian Celts and their language, religion and culture

As modern scientists have delved into the history of humankind they have discovered that our genes have changed very little through the long centuries. The genes of people from ancient civilizations continue right up to the present, so, like our ancestors, if they were Celts we continue to be Celts; it's in our genes. A recent branch of study called *Epigenetics* has been looking at the effects of both the physical characteristics that are passed down, and of catastrophic events that have occurred in our ancestors' lives. Surprisingly, they are finding that even the effects of catastrophic events can be inherited in our genes.

CELTIC CHARACTERISTICS

As we have seen, research has revealed that Celtic characteristics have not changed greatly. While we make astonishing leaps forward in industry, communication, and in many other facets of our lives, human nature itself seems to have changed very little and both personality and physical traits have been handed down from one generation to the next over thousands of years. In some ways, that is to be celebrated. If we have inherited a Celtic background we are probably programmed to be very creative, inventive and artistic. Remember those Celts of old? They were creative workers in bronze and gold, artists, talented musicians, beautiful singers, sensitive poets and good storytellers, always ready to tell or listen to a good yarn. They were loyal and hospitable.

On the other hand, we can be dismayed to find, if we are Celts, that we often have a mean streak, that we enjoy a

'good fight,' can be quarrelsome between ourselves, can turn the smallest event into a full-blown drama, can be very bossy and dictatorial in our dealings with each other, have strong love-hate relationships, do not always want to listen to advice, preferring to go our own way and we need to learn by making our own mistakes. We may come to faith as Christians, but then find that ancient superstitions seem to remain deep down and are difficult to eradicate.

In his *Letter to the Galatians* we find that Paul, in the time he spent with them, had really grown to know, understand and love his readers.

PAUL OF TARSUS
Named Saul, Paul was born in Tarsus, the capital city of the Roman Province of Celicia, now in south central Turkey. It was an ancient city, probably founded by the Greeks about six thousand years ago on the banks of the Cydnus. This river widened to form a safe harbour in the city centre, then continued for twenty kilometres to empty into the Mediterranean Sea.[2] The land was low-lying and the city had hot summers and cold, damp winters.

Tarsus was on the main line of communication between Anatolia and Syria and was a bustling place of commerce, known for its wealth, especially in the production and sale of linen and timber. Under the early Roman Emperors, Tarsus was also renowned as a place of education, having great schools that were considered equally as good as those of Athens and Alexandria.

SAUL'S EDUCATION
Saul's Jewish parents were Roman citizens but they ensured that he had a good Jewish education. This mainly centred on learning the Torah, the Old Testament Law, at home and in the synagogue.

As was the custom, formal education began when the child was five years old. Later, Saul travelled to Jerusalem to

---

[2] In 38 B.C. Cleopatra had sailed up the river from the Mediterranean for her famous meeting with Anthony.

continue his education under the learned Rabbi Gamaliel, grandson of Rabbi Hillel.

SAUL'S CONVERSION

Around 35 A.D., Saul had almost completed his studies when he witnessed the stoning of St. Stephen. Then he was commissioned by the high priest and the Sanhedrin to eradicate a community of Christians in Damascus. While travelling there with companions he was blinded by a light from Heaven. He fell to the ground and heard a voice saying: *"Saul, Saul, why are you persecuting me?"* This life-changing event is described in Acts 9. Briefly, his companions led him the rest of the way. In Damascus, Ananias, a Christian disciple, visited him, laid his hands on him and his sight was restored. He was baptized a Christian and renamed Paul.

After withdrawing for a time of meditation in the desert, Paul joined a group of other disciples who had been called to take Christianity to the Gentiles. He made three extensive missionary journeys in Asia Minor and Southern Europe over a number of years.

PAUL'S FIRST MISSIONARY JOURNEY

Barnabas, Paul, John Mark and some others travelled together to Galatia as part of what we now call Paul's first missionary journey.

We can read about this journey in St. Luke's second book, *The Acts of the Apostles*, chapters 13-14. Luke was a physician and often accompanied Paul on his missionary travels and he kept good records. He tells us that at first Barnabas was leader of the team that set off on the mission, but soon Paul took control. The group left Syrian Antioch, sailed to Cyprus to visit the home of Barnabas and then sailed to Perga in Pamphylia in Asia Minor. Here John Mark left the little group to return to Jerusalem.

The rest of the party then continued on foot to Galatia, beginning in Antioch in the region of Pisidia (Acts 13.14-52), walking on to Iconium (Acts 14.1-6), then to Lystra (Acts 14.6, 8-19) and later on to Derbe, in the Region of Lycaonia (Acts 14.6, 8-19).

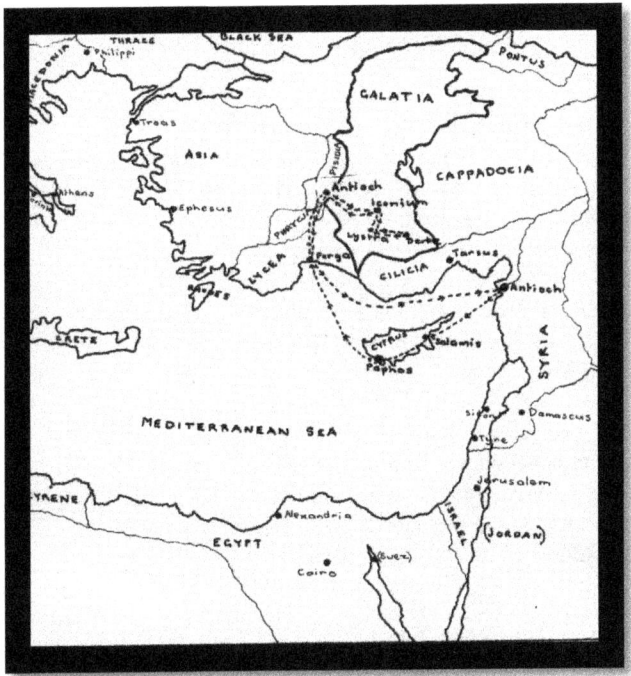

Map Showing Barnabas and Paul's First Missionary Journey

Eventually the team retraced their steps back to Lystra (14.21-23), through Iconium (Acts 14.14.21-23) and back to Antioch in Pisidia. Leaving from Attalia in Lycia they sailed back to their home base in Syrian Antioch (Acts 14.24). On this first missionary journey the group made a number of converts and most of these were Gentiles (Acts 13.44). The infant churches were set up with leaders and left to meet together to worship and to spread the faith.

Paul was eventually arrested, but as a Roman citizen he appealed to be brought before the Emperor Nero and was sent to Rome and imprisoned there. During his imprisonment, he wrote several letters to the churches that he had planted or visited during his travels. Finally, he was beheaded in the year 67 A.D. and the sword that was used later became recognized as his symbol. The Spanish Convent of La Lisla claims to possess the actual sword.

PAUL'S MEMORIAL

Paul's body was buried in Rome and at first a small memorial building was erected over his tomb. Over time, several basilicas were built on the site, the first in 324 A.D. This was extended and rebuilt and by the ninth century it had grown to be the largest church in Rome. In 1823 most of the church was burned down, although the cloisters, apse, arch and St. Paul's tomb all survived. By 1854 it had been rebuilt.

The new basilica includes an atrium that has a four-sided portico with seventy Corinthian columns. In the centre stands a large Carrara marble statue of St. Paul. The basilica is known as the church of St. Paolo Fuori le Mura, St. Paul Without the Walls.

THE BACKGROUND OF PAUL'S LETTER

The epistle, or letter, that Paul addressed to these fickle Celts is probably the first of his that has been preserved for us in the New Testament. It was addressed to '*the churches of Galatia*' (Galatians 1.2). Those churches were possibly house-churches and there must have been a number of them.

The leaders of each of the churches were probably people that Barnabas and Paul had converted. Later these leaders may have gone out into a number of the local communities where they lived and commenced new churches to add to those that Paul had begun. These churches all seem to have originated in the southern part of the Roman Province of Galatia as a result of the first missionary journey of Paul and his team (Acts 13.1-14.28). The cities that we know they visited in Galatia were Iconium, Lystra and Derbe. The whole journey was quite lengthy and it is believed that it took about a year and a half.

As we can read in *The Acts of the Apostles*, in some places where they conducted their mission they were very well received and many converts were made. In Galatia, they worked and lived for a time among the people and so learned just what they were like. Paul had even observed some fifteen of their worst characteristics when he had seen them living as heathen idol worshippers. Then many had accepted Jesus as their Saviour, and he loved them deeply as brothers and sisters in Christ and was concerned about them.

PROBLEMS IN THE GALATIAN CHURCH

Some time later, a problem arose that the leaders of the infant churches had difficulty coping with, and Paul, their missionary leader who had first led them to Christ was far away.

Much discussion, debate and gossiping had ensued between the churches' members ever since they had heard a new message from some visiting preachers. Who was right? Who had brought them the true message from God? In Celtic fashion, a big, dramatic fuss caused discord in the community and it unsettled everyone so much that some of the leaders wrote to Paul. He may even have received several letters alerting him to the problem caused by these visiting Jewish Christians who had upset the new converts.

The new preachers had introduced so much confusion among the people of the Galatian churches that things were in turmoil. The new Christians, even their leaders, did not know what to think about this message. Some reverted to what they knew, their old pagan worship. So the leaders hastily decided to write to Paul and tell him about what was happening in the Celtic churches. This letter was his reply. It was one of Paul's earliest letters and was written about 48 A.D., probably from his home church in Antioch in Syria before the Jerusalem Council (Acts 15.1-31) that was held about 49 A.D. to discuss Gentile membership in the church.

Paul's first mission was so early in his own Christian journey that he may not yet have learnt from the other Apostles all the precious details about Jesus' ministry, as in Paul's response there are no allusions to events that occurred during Jesus' life on earth and no direct quotes from the words of Jesus. There is one possible quote: '*Love your neighbour as yourself*' but this is also found in Leviticus 19.18. Paul knew this Book very well, as did Jesus, who was quoting from it when He made His famous summation of the Law (Luke 10.27). The Old Testament Scriptures were so familiar to Paul that he used many quotations and references with such ease that they appear almost seamless.

THE LANGUAGES OF THE BIBLE
Most of the Old Testament books, which constituted the Scriptures that the Jews, including Paul, and the other Apostles knew, were written in Hebrew, although Daniel and Ezra were in Aramaic, while parts of Genesis and Jeremiah also included Aramaic.

By the time of the New Testament writings, the Roman Empire had come to power, but Greek had remained the language of scholarship so the Gospels and the other books of the New Testament, which includes Paul's letter to the Galatians, were written in Greek. However, the first language of many of the writers was Aramaic and so we find a few words of that language creeping into the New Testament occasionally, including words of Jesus.

This fact suggests to us that the Galatians must have been accomplished linguists: they received, and presumably wrote letters in Greek, had interaction with the Roman rulers, so probably for their own security understood and spoke passable Latin, and we know that in their own homes they spoke their native Celtic language.[3]

Paul, too, must have spoken, written and read several languages. Since most of the Old Testament Scriptures that he studied were in Hebrew he must have known that language well, and also Aramaic. As he and his parents were Roman citizens, they would have been conversant with Latin as well. I wonder what he spoke when preaching to the Galatians?

---

[3] *See* Appendix 2

To Think About or Discuss

1. If you have Celtic ancestry, how do you think this has affected the way in which you think and act? If you do not have Celtic ancestry, can you find any differences between the way you think and act and the ways of your Celtic friends?

2. Do you think that the sword is a good symbol to represent Paul? Why?

3. How did the quote from Leviticus 19.18 differ from Jesus' reply? Was His reply reported in exactly the same way in all the gospels?

≈2≈

PAUL'S GREETING: PART I
CHAPTER 1. 1 - 2

Paul's introduction to his *Letter to the Galatians* commenced with a greeting or salutation. In the first two verses he began his letter in much the same way that he began his later letters that have been preserved for us in the New Testament.

THE FIRST TWO VERSES
1 ¹*Paul an apostle – not from men nor through man, but through Jesus Christ and God the Father, who raised him from the dead –* ²*and all the brothers who are with me,*
To the churches of Galatia:

When we receive a letter from a friend, we often try to discover the name of the sender from the style of handwriting on the envelope or on the letter itself. Otherwise we need to turn to the end of the letter to find the sender's signature. However, in Paul's time it was the tradition of his culture for the writer to put his own name first, and that is the way Paul begins.

PAUL'S AUTHORITY WAS FROM GOD
Paul's name was followed by his position or standing in the community. For Paul, it was his position in the hierarchy of the Christian church. Although he was not one of Jesus' close friends, the Twelve Apostles, as they were known, Paul claimed to be an Apostle. By using this word, he emphasized that his authority had come from God.

It appears that the false teachers who had come into the Galatian churches had been questioning Paul's authority, hinting, or even saying outright, that as he was not one of the original Twelve he was not a true Apostle, so right away at the very beginning of his letter he is replying to this innuendo to help straighten out any misconceptions. Paul points out what he had probably told the Galatians during his mission there: that he had not received the gospel from other people, not even the other Apostles, but as a direct revelation from God. By writing that he was not an Apostle *'from men or through man,'* Paul stressed that he had not been sent to them by any human authority and that he had not heard the gospel from the other Apostles, nor from anyone else, but that he had received it directly from God the Father and God the Son who had been crucified for their sins and was now alive.

PAUL WAS CALLED BY GOD

Paul was at great pains to stress to these confused Celts that his authorization was straight from God. He wrote that he was: *'an apostle ... through Jesus Christ and God the Father'* (1.1).

Although he may have been living and studying as a young man in Jerusalem at the time, he had not known or followed Jesus. Furthermore, he had not been chosen by the other leaders to be an Apostle, God chose him for this special position and He called Paul to go out and proclaim the gospel. He continued to pursue this line of thought and from it we learn these important points:
- Paul was an Apostle
- Paul's authority was from God, through Jesus Christ
- Paul's authority was endorsed by the Christians who were with him

In his opening statement Paul was making a direct appeal to the Galatians to accept his letter and the message it brought. He supported his position by emphasizing this three-fold authority for his ministry. God Himself had called Paul. By writing this, he provided the strongest defence possible in order to emphasize the truth and importance of the original message that he had preached to these Celtic people. This defence continued right until Chapter 2.21 and included reference to three of the most influential Twelve Apostles, James, Cephas and John (Gal. 2.9). In Galatians 2.11-22, Paul stressed his authority by mentioning his correction of Cephas (for more on Cephas v Peter, *see* footnote on page 54).

Paul told the Galatians that they were wrong in thinking that the gospel demanded that they should be circumcised in order to gain salvation. This was what these new teachers had been telling them. In typical fashion, the Celts had probably offered their famous hospitality to these new itinerant preachers, had politely listened to what their guests had to say, as their tradition demanded, and now they were in a quandary. The message of these visiting preachers was based on Jewish legalism and was completely anti-Christian. It was contrary to what Barnabas, Paul and his friends had taught and Paul urgently wanted his readers to understand this: the risen Christ Himself had revealed His message to Paul.

A DIGRESSION

At this point it could be useful to pause for a moment and explore the meaning of some of the words that Paul used, to help us to understand the difference between them as they can sometimes be confusing: *Disciple*, *Apostle* and *Missionary*.

1. **THE WORD 'DISCIPLE'**
   Going back to Paul's introduction of himself as an Apostle, it is interesting to note that in *Matthew*, we find in Chapter 10.1, Jesus' special group of chosen followers are described as '*his twelve disciples.*'

This word, '*disciple*,' comes from a Latin word that means '*learner*' and refers to all the followers of Jesus. However, the inner group of twelve disciples Jesus chose early in His ministry became His special friends and supporters, as well as learners. Sometimes we apply the word 'disciple' to ourselves as well.[4] As Christians, we are followers of Jesus, but we are not one of the specially chosen Twelve.

2. THE WORD 'APOSTLE'

If we read on further in Matthew we notice that in the very next verse they are described as' Apostles.' What happened in this short time? Jesus had given His Twelve Disciples authority to be His representatives and to be sent out to the "*lost sheep of Israel*" (Matthew 10.6), that is, to the Jews, not the Gentiles, which would have included the Galatians.

The word '*apostle*' is a Greek word that means '*messenger*.' It especially refers to the twelve disciples that Jesus chose as his close group from the many people who followed Him.[5]

Why this change of name? In Matthew 10.24, the word '*disciple*' is still being used. We find the reason in Luke 6.13 where we are told that Jesus went out to the mountain and prayed all night, then, '*When day came, he called his disciples and*

---

[4] The word '*disciple*' is found 29 times in the New Testament. The plural '*disciples*' appears only once in the Old Testament, in Isaiah 8.16, but it is found 244 times in the New Testament.

[5] The word '*apostle*' is not found in the Old Testament, although it is found 29 times in the New Testament and the plural, '*apostles*' is found 60 times, but again, only in the New Testament.

chose from them twelve, whom he named apostles.'

As we saw, this word comes from the Greek and that was the language of learning and education. Actually there was a much larger group of disciples; they were the men and women who followed Jesus because they wanted to learn more about God. This is explained also in Mark 3.13. There were many who were disciples of Jesus, but only twelve whom Jesus chose to be Apostles, His special messengers.

So what about Paul? Could he really claim to be an apostle of Jesus? Remember that after the crucifixion and resurrection there was a gap, as Judas Iscariot had left the team. The Twelve represented the twelve tribes of Israel and it had been foretold in Psalms that another would be chosen to take his place.[6] The eleven faithful Apostles who remained cast lots to choose another from two of the disciples who had been with them from the time of John's baptizing until the resurrection, and Matthias was chosen (Acts 1.26). Three others were added to the group of apostles a little later: Paul, Barnabas, and James, the brother of Jesus. Although Paul had studied the Law in far more detail than the other Apostles, his special call was to the Gentiles, and in this letter, that means the Galatians, the Gauls living in Galatia.

What significance does this have for us today? We are followers of Christ and love to gather together to worship Him and learn more about Him. We are His disciples, but we call ourselves

---

[6] Acts 1.20, which quotes firstly Psalm 69.25: "*May his camp become desolate, and let there be no one to dwell in it,*" followed by Psalm 109.8: "*Let another take his office.*"

Christians.[7] Christian is the word that has been used since shortly after this Letter was written. It means believers and those who have been baptized in Christ's name.

In some churches we still use the word 'apostle' when we speak of the 'Apostolic Succession,' those who, like the Twelve Apostles, have been ordained as Christ's messengers to the world.

3. **THE WORD 'MISSIONARY'**
There is also another word we use today: 'missionary.' It means a person sent on a journey for a religious assignment to spread the faith. The Galatian churches that Paul addresses had been founded on his first missionary journey. He had been sent, as we Christians today are 'sent' as missionaries, whether it is to our neighbours at home, or to lands far away. This word 'missionary' is a newer word; it is not found in either the Old Testament or the New Testament.

PAUL'S SUPPORTERS

Paul continued in verse two: '*and all the brothers who are with me.*' Another translation is more inclusive: '*and all the members of God's family who are with me.*' Paul called those who were with him brothers and sister in the family of God, the Christians of his home church in Antioch in Syria.

He backed up his words by writing that those with him in the home church agreed with the veracity of the message

---

[7] The word 'Christian' is only found twice in the infant Church as described in the New Testament, in Acts 26.28 and in 1Peter 4.16; the plural is even more rare as it is only found once, in Acts 11.26. Both of these were written later than when Paul wrote Galatians, so at this time it was not a word in common usage.

that he proclaimed when their team stayed with the Galatians. Already Paul was beginning to address the problem that the Galatians were facing. All those with him agreed that the gospel he and Barnabas preached to them was the correct one; it was straight from God.

As we have seen, the opening verses of Paul's letter contain his greeting or salutation. In it he wrote that his letter came from all the Christians who were with him and that he was sending the letter to all the churches in Galatia. We do not know if it was copied out several times by hand[8] or if it was read aloud to one congregation and then passed on to the next. However we do know that it was considered precious as it was preserved until the middle of the third century when the New Testament was completed.

---

[8] There were no means of printing in those days

To Think About or Discuss

1. Should Paul be referred to as an apostle or as a disciple? (This question can be answered in different ways).

2. In this 'politically correct' age how comfortable are you with a translation that uses the masculine when all people are addressed?

3. How can we know that we are 'called by God?'

4. In Luke 6.13 we read that Jesus went out to the mountain and prayed all night.
   Discuss the importance of prayer for Jesus.
   - Did He do this very often?
   - How important is prayer in our own lives?
   - How important should it be?

≈3≈

PAUL'S GREETING: PART II
CHAPTER 1. 3 - 5

Traditional introductions were quite often longer than these first five verses. However, although Paul's introduction in this letter was comparatively brief, he emphasized to his confused Galatian readers that he wanted them to understand that his mission and preaching was not simply some idea of his own, but that he had been chosen by God to do this work. He stressed that he has the support of the other Christians who were with him at the time of writing. He had been chosen as God's messenger and sent to announce the Good News to the Gentiles, and here, especially to these erstwhile heathen Galatians, to remind them of the wonderful new life in Jesus they had chosen.

GRACE AND PEACE

1 *³Grace to you and peace from God our Father and the Lord Jesus Christ, ⁴who gave himself for our sins to deliver us from the present evil age, according to the will of our God and Father, ⁵to whom be the glory forever and ever. Amen.*

The traditional introduction that Paul began in verses 1 and 2 continued as he wished all the Christian churches in Galatia grace and peace (1.3) by reminding them that their conversion was according to God's will and part of His wonderful plan for them.

GOD'S GRACE

God's grace is different from our earthly idea of grace; we often think of someone who moves gracefully, or is gracious in the way they act towards others. God's grace is His free and unearned (and definitely unmerited) favour; it is His kindness and mercy towards us, His children. How blessed we are that we can avail ourselves of the wonderful grace of both God our Father and the Lord Jesus Christ! Of ourselves we certainly cannot earn this grace, nor, as sinners are we worthy to receive it, and yet it is free for those who believe and seek His favour. Paul blesses the Galatians with God's grace.

GOD'S PEACE

When the world thinks of peace it usually means the absence of war. This thinking even covers the notion of peace within families; peace from the bickering and quarrelling that we Celts often seem to indulge in. As Paul began to deal with the uproar that was going on among the Galatians it seemed that even the absence of war would be a good thing in these volatile communities where everyone had an opinion and did not hesitate to voice it.

God's peace is Jesus' peace: *'peace from God our Father and the Lord Jesus Christ'* (1.3). Later, when John wrote his Gospel while he was exiled on the island of Patmos, he quoted those memorable words of Jesus: *'Not as the world gives, give I unto you'* (John 14. 27).

God's peace is true peace that goes to the depth of our hearts and beings. It reminds us of the Old Testament understanding of peace where it concerns each individual, but also embraces the whole community. The wellbeing of the people was blessed as they sought a right relationship with God[9]. It is because of that right relationship with God, both Father and Son, that he gives us His peace.

Paul was showing his deep love for these new converts in giving them this wonderful blessing. It fitted in with their Celtic culture, but notice that here there is no thanksgiving

---

[9] *See* Numbers 6.24-26

for their faith, hope and love that Paul usually included in his greetings in the introductions to his later letters.

True grace and peace can only come from '*God our Father and the Lord Jesus Christ.*' Here Paul made himself one with the Galatians by using the word '*our*' Father. Although they have strayed in their thinking, he still loved and accepted them as his fellow brothers and sisters, children of the Father.

THE GREETING OF PEACE

If we greet one another, it should be in grace and peace, too. When we 'pass the peace' and greet each other in church, it is from one Christian to another brother or sister in Christ. Notice that there is a special place in the service when we do this. The liturgy has been carefully designed so that we have first prayed for forgiveness of our sins through the precious sacrifice of Jesus on the cross. Then we have been purified, released from those sins so that we are made holy. Only then can we come to our Father God Who is so holy and make peace with Him.

After this, having made peace with God, we can make peace with each other. How beautiful is that! It is not a time to remind a friend about that return game of tennis or the children's party next week, it is a holy time of sharing God's peace with our brothers and sisters. If we have done something against them this could be a time to ask for forgiveness, and make our peace with that person, before sharing together at the Lord's Table later in the service.

See how well this step in the sequence of the service has been placed? The liturgy, the order of service, has surely been inspired by the Holy Spirit, designed especially for our spiritual well-being and the growth of our fellowship with God. Our greeting of each other is part of our worship of our Heavenly Father.

GALATIAN CULTURE AND PEACE

Let us think for a moment about the Galatians and their culture. They had been nomads until comparatively recently. They were pagans who put their babies out in the cold weather to make them tough. If they survived, they were kept, if not, they died. Perhaps that is where my mother got her ideas from; she insisted on our swimming in the sea every school holidays, even in winter, to make us tougher. That was something we did not appreciate.

The Celts were great storytellers, enjoying reminiscences of past events that involved their ancestors. Only three hundred years before, the disastrous 'Elephant Battle'[10] had taken place. The Celts had been confronted by the huge, strange creatures. They had been terrified, aghast, and had completely 'lost it' - and lost the battle. Stories about this were still told. Only a hundred years before Barnabas and Paul's mission, the Galatians continued to raid the surrounding areas. This behaviour was part of their culture, and was certainly not conducive to peace, nor did it make them welcome in the surrounding communities.

The Celtic culture of the Galatians also contributed to their downfall. Hospitality, given and received, was very important to them. Their foes utilized this characteristic to take unfair advantage. Mithridates IV invited sixty of the Galatian chiefs to meet him at Pergamum and the Galatians accepted the invitation. It was a cunning ruse and all were massacred except one chief who managed to escape. The remaining Galatians were lost without their leaders and became despondent. They lost a lot of their spirit and went over to the Roman side.[11]

By the time that the missionary team arrived in Galatia, the Greek influence from their past was still evident and the architecture of some of the Galatian cities continued to be

---

[10] *See* Appendix 1, 275-4 B.C.
[11] *See* Appendix 1, 88 B.C.

seen in the Hellenistic building techniques used. However, the Celtic influence also remained and their fortified sites were typical Celtic hill forts. Over time the Galatians gradually absorbed Roman ways, but along with these influences, they continued to retain most of their ethnic identity. Although they had learned both the Greek and Roman languages, by the time that Paul wrote his letter, presumably in Greek, they still used their Gallic language among themselves. The Christian ethics of grace and peace that Paul taught were very new ideas for these Celts.

CHRIST CRUCIFIED

Jesus Christ, who came to live as a human being among us, the one and only person who had never sinned, *'gave himself for our sins'* (1. 4). He sacrificed His life for all humankind, so that we could be set free, unfettered from all that held us back so that we could be changed and made acceptable to Father God and enter the joy of eternal life in His presence. The death of the sinless One so that sinful humankind could have life! What a sacrifice! I think of Jesus' prayer in the Garden of Gethsemane before Judas and the soldiers came, *'Father, if you are willing remove this cup from me. Nevertheless, not my will, but yours, be done'* (Luke 22.42). He was obedient to His Father's will, even to suffering a painful and ignominious death.

How often when we were children, and even now as adults, do we seethe with 'righteous indignation' if we are accused of doing some wrongful act, when we know that we are innocent? I remember taking quite a beating from my mother for something I had not done, but no way was I going to betray my young sister. How much more dreadful for Jesus Christ, who had never sinned and yet received the death sentence, betrayed by one of His inner group of friends. This is the main point of Paul's letter: Jesus saves people from their sins and sets them free. What were the Galatians set free from? And bringing it to the present, what are we set free from?

SET FREE FROM THE EVILS OF THE PRESENT AGE

'The Lord Jesus Christ ... gave himself for our sins to deliver us from the present evil age' (1.4a). If we are not set free, delivered from the evils of our age, then we remain slaves to those evils and there is no true freedom. It was the same *'evil age'* for the Galatians as it is for us today. Paul was obviously upset by the attitude of these Celts who were showing how prone they were to sudden changes of mood and allegiance, how swayed they were by what he could see were the evil intentions of these false teachers. This *'present evil age'* continues to be evil and there are people everywhere with evil intent.

Where was the Celts' newfound faith, their hope of life everlasting that he had brought them, or their love for the other members of their infant churches? They had welcomed these visiting preachers with their traditional and renowned hospitality, and had listened politely to their message as behoved good Celts. But this message was not the same as Paul's. At this first cold blast from outsiders they succumbed. They were thoroughly confused and unable to distinguish who was right: Paul or these new preachers. Whose message was truly from God? The Galatian churches were in turmoil.

Paul reminded the Galatians that although they were in the world, they were not of the world; through Jesus, they had found faith in God and now belonged to Him. The world around them was sinful, in fact downright evil in many ways and would try to entice them away from their newly chosen path, but with God's help they must learn to differentiate between true and false and turn away from sin.

Only through Jesus' sacrifice when He *'gave himself for our sins'* (1.4) on the cross could the Galatians be made holy and approach the throne of Almighty God and gain forgiveness. He is so holy that this is the only way He can forgive their sins, and it remains the only way for us today.

THE WILL OF OUR GOD AND FATHER

Paul added, '*According to the will of our God and Father*' (1.4b). It was God's will that these Celts would be freed from the seductive influence of the world to which they had been enslaved.

It is the same today, whether we are Celts or any other culture. We aim to live according to God's will for our lives. We often fail, but we continue to strive towards that goal. When we pray, we often ask for things we are unsure about, that we may want, but not really need. Then we can also pray that we are only given these things if it is according to our Father's will for us.

The way that Paul referred to God as '*our* God and Father' is telling. He was truly angry with the false preachers and disappointed that the Galatians had listened and allowed themselves to be led astray. However, they were but 'babes in Christ' and Paul was not casting them off because they had strayed. By writing that God is 'our' Father, he showed that he continued to count them as brother and sister Christians who had just been inveigled onto the wrong path. He still shared with them and loved them as the Father's children. He was concerned for their welfare and deeply desired that they followed the right path.

CONCLUSION OF PAUL'S GREETING

Paul concluded his greeting: '*to whom be the glory for ever and ever*' (1.5). The Galatians, all Celts and all people through the ages, can be released from our sins and made pure and holy to have fellowship with the Father and give God the glory for all eternity! What a wonderful conclusion to Paul's greeting!

These five verses are the only introduction. In some of his other letters, we find longer greetings that praise God for the people's faithfulness, but when writing to these Celts, Paul was upset by their behavior and kept it brief. Faith and trust in God lead towards maturity in Christ. Paul developed this theme further in his letter, especially in Chapter 3.22-26 and in Chapter 4.1-11.

In response and thanks for this great gift of freedom that they had gained through the death and resurrection of Jesus Christ, Paul and the Galatians showed their gratitude and gave God the glory. They - and we - can praise Him for release from slavery to the evils of the world. To God be the glory!

To Think About or Discuss

1. In his letter, Paul wrote that he had been:
   - ***chosen*** as God's messenger
   - ***sent*** to announce the Good News to the Gentiles
   - ***called*** to remind the Galatians of the wonderful new life in Jesus that they had already chosen.

   Do you think that these Celts had chosen their new life or that God had chosen them?
   Did you choose God or did He choose you?

2. How do we react if we are accused of a wrongdoing and know that we are innocent? How should we react?

3. Discuss Paul's statement about *'the present evil age'* (1.4). He wrote that about two thousand years ago. Is the present age today as evil as it was then? If it has changed, how has that come about?

≈4≈

PAUL'S REASON FOR WRITING: CHAPTER 1. 6 - 9

Verses 6–9, now turn to Paul's reason for writing. These verses encapsulate the main theme that the letter was to follow and what had happened to give him the occasion for writing. He was greatly upset at the Galatians' lapse from the gospel that God had brought them through his preaching and that of his travelling companions. He stressed that there could never be another gospel.

1 *⁶I am astonished that you are so quickly deserting him who called you in the grace of Christ and are turning to a different gospel – ⁷not that there is another one, but there are some who trouble you and want to distort the gospel of Christ. ⁸But even if we, or an angel from heaven, should preach to you a gospel contrary to the one we preached to you, let him be accursed! ⁹As we have said before, so now I say again: If anyone is preaching to you a gospel contrary to the one you received, let him be accursed.*

Paul was amazed that this change of belief and attitude had happened to the Galatians so quickly after he and the team had left them. It was comparatively such a brief length of time since they had accepted the gospel of Christ, and now, through the visit of some itinerant preachers, they were questioning it. He then expressed his condemnation of the incorrect preaching by Christian Jews to Celts who are not Jews, but Gentiles.

DESERTERS

In these verses, Paul cut straight to the purpose of his letter. As we read, he curtailed the traditional greeting and omitted the usual thanksgiving. This omission would have been very obvious to those who read his letter. They understood the cultural traditions and it was quite obvious that Paul was upset; he had not wasted time and parchment[12] on niceties. He wanted it to be glaringly obvious to the Galatians just how he felt. He angrily labelled them deserters (1.6) and in anyone's language that is a serious insult. He wanted to grab their full attention so that they grasped the critical implications of why he was writing to them.

Paul had a great mind and was aware of the background of these Celts; he had lived among them, eaten with them, worked with them and laughed with them. Most likely, as they sat around the fires in the evenings he had listened to their stories. After all, it was only about a hundred years earlier that they had changed their allegiance and gone over to the side of the Romans. In fact, they had quite a history of changing over to whichever side was going to be to their own advantage. They would not have missed the import of this reference in the opening part of his letter.

I wonder: are we ever deserters? Do we run away from difficult situations, hoping that they will simply disappear? Only they don't, do they? Even Jesus in the Garden of Gethsemane prayed that God would remove the bitter cup that He knew lay before Him. But He did not run away, He stayed and faced that dreadful, painful death. His sacrifice, His death on the cross was the only way that our sins could

---

[12] Paul wrote his letters on either parchment or papyrus. Papyrus was a kind of paper made from reeds while parchment was made from skins, usually the skins of sheep, which had been treated and made quite thin and pliable. The other possibility was vellum, which was finer and made from the skins of calves and lambs, but that was more expensive.

The ink that people used on parchment in those times was made of gum or oil mixed with black carbon; for papyrus the base was mixed with a metallic material. The pen was like a quill pen, made from a reed that was cut to a point that was split.

be forgiven. Through it we can be made holy so that we are able to enter into fellowship with our Heavenly Father. And that is so important to us as Christians.

FELLOWSHIP WITH THE FATHER

When we have fellowship with the Father, we talk with Him in a variety of ways: in prayer, praise and in meditation, and what joy we can receive through these.

- **Prayers for Forgiveness**:
  When we pray for forgiveness through the sacrifice of Jesus Christ, it is for both the wrong things we have done, our *sins of commission*, and for the things we should have done and did not, our *sins of omission*.

- **Prayers of Intercession**:
  We ask our Father and make our petitions for things big and small, for healing, for blessing, for ourselves, for our neighbours, for peace and love, for safety and for the work of the Holy Spirit among all people and nations around the world.

- **Praise**:
  We praise Almighty God in gratitude for His great goodness to all humankind. There is so much that we can praise God for, with all the fullness of our hearts. When we are feeling 'down,' praise lifts us up to the great **I AM**.

- **Meditation**:
  A quiet time alone with God, takes us apart from the busyness of the world. It is important to withdraw and make time to ponder on the wonder of His love for us, and think with grateful hearts about all that He means to us.

Jesus did not desert what He knew was ahead, but faced it, terrible as it was. When difficulties occur in our lives, as they inevitably will, we should not run away from them either. With Jesus as our example, we should pray and face our problems, knowing that He understands and that the Holy Spirit will teach us and strengthen us. In the end, we will be stronger for the experience. Remember that God does not allow us to face anything more than He knows we can bear, even if sometimes it does not seem like that at the time. God is with us, so who can be against us?

THERE IS NO OTHER GOSPEL
Very little time had elapsed since Paul and the team introduced these Celts to Jesus Christ. The listeners had embraced the good news, the gospel, and readily became followers of Jesus, joining with others to form new churches in Southern Galatia. Their desertion from the faith had occurred '*so quickly*' (Galatians 1.6); so soon they had been thrown into confusion by visiting preachers who were teaching a '*different gospel.*' These new Christians were turning this way and that and did not know whom to believe.

The Galatians were abandoning the true gospel. As we have seen, some strangers had arrived and were preaching a different message. They were attracting the people away from the truths that they had learned from Paul and the team. Paul feels deserted by these people who had accepted him and the message that he brought from God. He cared deeply for the salvation of these pagan Celts and had taught them to love and care about God and His will for them and the way they lived their lives. If they followed the path these false preachers advocated, they faced apostasy, the abandonment of all the Christian beliefs they had embraced under Paul's teaching.

OUR RELATIONSHIP WITH GOD

How often we, too, can backslide or be enticed to step onto the wrong path instead of seeking God's will in our lives. We need to go back and relearn to *care about what we know about Him and know about what we care about Him.* That may sound trite, but it is very deep. It is important for us, if we care about God and the gospel to know as much as we can about Him and the Scriptures. Look at it the other way: if we have given our lives to God we need to know as much as we can about Him and learn how to have true fellowship with Him. If we study God's Word and learn more about our great Heavenly Father, then we will care more about improving and retaining our relationship with Him each day, too.

There's a story that goes something like this:

A lady went to a famous doctor to consult him about her health. She had many troubles that caused her to be so stressed she was making herself ill. She listed all her symptoms to the doctor and answered his questions, but was astonished at his prescription.
He said,
"Madam, you need to read the Bible more."
"But doctor," the patient began.
"Go home and read your Bible for an hour every day," the great man told her, "then come back in a month's time."
He bowed her out before she could say more.

At first, the woman was angry. Then she reflected that it was not a difficult prescription. It had been a long time since she had read her Bible regularly. She went home and decided to follow the prescription. In a month she returned to the doctor.

"Well," he smiled, "I see that you have been obedient and have followed my prescription. Do you need any other medicine now?"

"No, doctor," she replied, "I feel like a different person. But how did you know what I needed?"

The doctor turned to his desk. On it, lay an open Bible, marked and worn.

"Madam," he said earnestly, "If I were to omit my daily reading of this Book I would lose my greatest source of strength and skill. I never operate without finding help in its pages. You did not need medicine, but a source of peace outside yourself. I gave you my own prescription and knew it would cure you."

"I very nearly didn't try it," she confessed.

"Few are willing to try, but it would work wonders if they did."

In these three verses of Galatians 1.6-9, Paul stressed that although it seemed as if the Galatians were turning to a different gospel, in reality there *was* no other gospel. Either they believed in the gospel that he taught and put their faith and trust in Christ Jesus, or they reverted to being the idol worshippers they had been before they met Paul.

THE GOSPEL

Let us look for a moment at this word 'gospel.' We use it often and sometimes rather glibly, but what does it mean? It comes from the Old English and simply means 'good news,' but that encompasses everything that matters.

The good news that Paul brought these Celts was that Jesus, the only Son of God, came to the world as a human being to declare to humankind God's saving grace, His salvation. Only through accepting the sacrifice of Jesus, can these Galatians to whom Paul was writing be saved and attain eternal life. Paul pointed out that this message of good news was the only truth and there could be no other. Anything else was a perversion of the truth and should be utterly rejected. He wrote: *'there are some who trouble you and want to distort the gospel of Christ'* (1.7).

ANGELS FROM HEAVEN
Paul was really upset. He wrote that even if *'an angel from heaven'* (1.8) announced a different gospel, he would curse it.

For Paul and his contemporaries angels were real beings. The angels who serve God are mentioned in the Old Testament one hundred and four times and in the New Testament ninety-seven times, and the Old Testament was the Scripture of the Apostles. Angels had been a reality for God's people since the beginning. God created Adam and Eve and they knew of the existence of these spiritual beings. There were many records of their activities as they served God as His messengers. The Jews were also aware that there were both good and bad angels.[13]

Many of us only use the word in praise of someone who is seen as beautiful and good, but angels are real beings, or Jesus would not have referred to them. They played an important part in both the Old and New Testaments and are still at work today.

PAUL CURSED THOSE WHO LED ASTRAY
In verse 9 Paul reiterated: *'As we have said before, so now I say again: If anyone is preaching to you a gospel contrary to the one you received, let him be accursed.'* He made it quite evident that he was extremely upset and angry. After all his effort in building good relationships with these Celts and leading them to new life in Christ, a group of itinerant preachers had infiltrated their ranks. Instead of confirming the Good News that Paul had taught, these preachers had stirred up the new converts, these

---

[13] Good angels: I Samuel 29.9; bad angels, Psalm 78.49; angels of the underworld: Matthew 25.41: *'the eternal fire prepared for the devil and his angels;'* 2 Peter 2.4: *'God did not spare angels when they sinned, but cast them into hell.'*

infants in Christ, so much that it had led to great dissension and confusion.

Twice in a short time, Paul called down God's curse on these bearers of false news. Firstly, he cursed any heavenly angel who would dare to bring an incorrect message from God, pretending that it is true. Secondly, He called down God's curse on these evildoers, the visiting preachers who were stirring up so much mischief among the new followers of Jesus, and were trying to lead them astray.

CURSING AND SWEARING

These curses of Paul's would have had quite an impact on the erstwhile superstitious Celts. I've often wondered what kind of curses Paul would have used, apart from these words. He was so well versed in the Law of Moses that it most certainly would not have been breaking the Law and taking the Lord's Name in vain as so many do today.

I don't know about you, but I feel it deeply when friends and even ministers use the name of the Lord in the wrong way; it really hurts. When I was young, most of the people I knew would never have said, "Oh, God!" or "Jesus!" without having any thought of God at all. I must admit that we did use lots of slang and colourful ways of expressing ourselves and our frustrations - frequently and on many different occasions, but we did not take the Lord's name in vain as some people do today. There's a difference between cursing someone and swearing. Cursing can be swearing, but it can also mean appealing to God to deal with the situation, even to the extent of eliminating the cause of the problem. Swearing, in this context, means using language that is offensive to God.

FALSE TEACHERS TODAY

How does this message affect us? We do not need to address this particular problem of circumcision and the

Law in our own church family but there are other problems that require consideration.

We can ask ourselves:
- Is the preaching that we hear each week according to the gospel?
- Is it in accordance with what the Bible teaches?
- If it is not, or if we are unsure, what will we do about it?

To do nothing infers that we agree with what is being taught. In a later letter to Timothy, Paul wrote: *'Whoever ... does not agree with the sound words of our Lord Jesus Christ and the teaching that accords with godliness, he is puffed up with conceit and understands nothing'* (1 Timothy 6.3-4a).

What can we do in such a situation?
- Firstly, we should not chat among ourselves, gossiping and complaining about the teaching. That will achieve nothing except unhappy people.
- Secondly, we can speak privately with the preacher and gently point out any teaching that does not agree with that of Jesus and the Scriptures.
- Thirdly, if this is not heeded, we can find some other like-minded people and go to the preacher as a concerned group.

I remember how embarrassed we were as teenagers when we had a visiting preacher who had already made some points that were not in accordance with the words of Jesus. Mother squirmed in her seat. Eventually it was too much for her. She stood up and said,
"Excuse me, Sir! Will you please stick to what the Bible tells us? I cannot have our young people's minds being exposed to such drivel."

All eyes were turned on her and we wished the ground would open up and swallow us. Was she right? What would you have done?

Through Paul's visit Paul these unruly Celts had turned to God; they had become a new people, His people, and a people of peace. That was a mighty about-turn for this quarrelsome lot of heathens, a real miracle. Was it all for nothing? Had it all been undone?

To Think About or Discuss

1 Was Paul right in feeling so upset that his converts had turned away from what he had taught them?

2 Angels are often mentioned in the Bible. Are they real beings? Discuss.

3 How would you react if your minister taught something that you thought was not consistent with the Scriptures?

≈5≈

PAUL'S STORY
CHAPTER 1. 10 – 16

Now Paul began to tell his faith story, starting with the Paul that the Galatians knew, and then going back to how he was before his conversion.

1 *^{10}For am I now seeking the approval of man, or of God? Or am I trying to please man? If I were still trying to please man, I would not be a servant of Christ. ^{11}For I would have you know, brothers, that the gospel that was preached by me is not man's gospel. ^{12}For I did not receive it from any man, nor was I taught it, but I received it through a revelation of Jesus Christ. ^{13}For you have heard of my former life in Judaism, how I persecuting the church of God violently and tried to destroy it. ^{14}And I was advancing in Judaism beyond many of my own age among my people, so extremely zealous was I for the traditions of my fathers. ^{15}But when he, who set me apart before I was born and who called me by his grace, ^{16}was pleased to reveal his Son to me, in order that I might preach him among the Gentiles, I did not immediately consult with anyone.*

Often we, as Christians, have an opportunity to tell our story to non-Christians, in the hope that they will come to understand the great contrast between the two stages of our lives. We hope that the listeners will relate this to their own lives and learn what a difference it makes when we hand our lives over to God and He is in charge of our journey.

PAUL'S CONVERSION
Paul described the result of his conversion that occurred when he and a group of Jewish zealots were travelling on their way to Damascus. He had been armed with letters from the high priest and the group intended to arrest any

Christians that they found in the synagogues there, men or women, bind them, and take them to Jerusalem (Acts 9.11-2). When the group had almost reached Damascus, he was halted by a dazzling light, and met the risen Christ (Acts 9.3-8). Blinded, he was led the rest of the way. For three days he remained blind, and fasted and prayed until God restored his sight through *'a disciple named Ananias'* (Acts 9.10) and then *'he rose and was baptized'* (Acts 9.18).

Through the grace of God Paul completely changed. He was young and had formerly worked hard with a group of like-minded young men determined to exterminate the Christians and to impress important and influential people in the upper echelons of the Jewish hierarchy.

PAUL'S NEW LIFE
Since God's revelation, all had changed; Paul was no longer a people pleaser. He asked: *'Am I now seeking the approval of man, or of God? Or am I trying to please man? If I were still trying to please man, I would not be a servant of Christ'* (1.10).

After his conversion Paul's goals changed. In earlier times when he had been persecuting the Christians he had strived to impress the Jewish leaders, but since then his whole life had been turned around. His only goal now was to please God. He had become a servant of Jesus Christ and do what Christ told him; he must obey what God was telling him in his heart, regardless of what other people might think and say, even those in high places who wielded great influence. Paul was being as positive as he possibly could.

We can look at this statement and read it as if it is our own confirmation of our attitude and the way we live. We can ask: 'Am I like that? Am I a true servant of Christ? Do I aim to please Him alone and not other people?' In current parlance, a *gratitude attitude* is a far better way to live. Gratitude to our Heavenly Father that we are freed from constantly wondering what others may think about our words and actions. Often, what other people around me might think and say can influence my speech and actions until these words of Paul come to my mind and pull me up short. What God thinks about us, and our relationship with Him is all that matters, and for that we can be grateful for such freedom. Paul had become very strong after his meeting with Jesus. We have a great model to follow.

PAUL'S DEFENCE
It appears that Paul's critics had claimed that he was teaching a gospel[14] he had only heard from others, as he had not known Jesus when He was on earth. *'I would have you know, brothers, that the gospel that was preached by me is not man's gospel. [12] For I did not receive it from any man, nor was I taught it, but I received it through a revelation of Jesus Christ'* (1.11-12).

Certainly, before his conversion Paul had been persecuting Jesus' followers with great vigour. The faultfinders implied that, because of this, not only was he not a true Apostle, but his message was not from God. Paul defended himself, but also showed a pastoral concern in the way he called the Galatians 'brothers and sisters' in some translations. He showed that he identified himself with his Celtic converts and, in this way, he reassured them that the gospel they had heard from him and the team was authentic.

HEARING THE GOSPEL
Unless we have experienced a vision as Paul did, we have not heard the gospel directly from Jesus Christ, either. We have heard it from our parents, our teachers or from other Christians. We need to be careful that the messages we

---

[14] Gospel: the word comes from the Anglo-Saxon *godspell*, meaning the story of God; it is a translation of the Greek word *evangelion*, which means 'the good story.'

hear and those we share with others are straight from God through scripture. Later Paul wrote in a letter to Timothy: *'All Scripture is breathed out by God and profitable for teaching, for reproof, for correction, and for training in righteousness'* (2 Timothy 3.16).

The Scriptures were Paul's guidebook and they are ours, too, but we are doubly blessed, as our Scriptures include the New Testament. I am reminded of the Rev. Simeon Busia, a dear old Papuan preacher. He preached straight from the *Buki Tabu*, the Holy Bible, and did not pull any punches when dealing with problems in the community. I remember him once reading a long Gospel passage in a very dramatic fashion. Then I realized he was holding his Bible upside down. He had no spectacles and was unable to read those precious words, but it did not matter. He had memorized them so well that he could recite them!

I wonder how many of us today could quote long passages from anywhere in the Bible. 'Learning by heart' is not so popular any more and sometimes we think it is unnecessary when we have our Bible with us on our laptops, ipads, tablets and iphones and can refer to them almost instantly. But 'heart' is the important word here – when we learn by heart we don't just store those words in our heads, they become part of us, part of our hearts, our very inner beings.

Once I heard a speaker who had been released from a concentration camp. He had been through some dreadful experiences, including what was called 'brain-washing.' Apparently his jailers had managed to cause him to forget almost everything, except what he had learned of the Word of God. That remained and it was that which sustained him.

PAUL'S EARLIER LIFE
Paul referred to his former life in Judaism, the religion of the Jews: *'You have heard of my former life in Judaism, how I persecuted the church of God violently and tried to*

destroy it. And I was advancing in Judaism beyond many of my own age among my people, so extremely zealous was I for the traditions of my fathers' (1.13-14).

As he wrote later in Romans (11.1), Paul proudly retained his identity as an Israelite, a descendant of Abraham and a member of the tribe of Benjamin. When he was writing in the first century A.D., rabbinic teaching was the foundation of Jewish life. In Mark (7.3-5) we read that the Pharisees kept strictly to the traditions of their forefathers, including the fact that when they came home from the marketplace if they didn't wash, they did not eat.

Paul described how, before he became a Christian, he had great zeal for maintaining his ancestors' traditions, outstripping many of his equals. However, as we know, he had now changed from attempting to achieve righteousness through the Law of Moses and his forebears' traditions. While he was living with the Galatians he abandoned some of his Jewish practices. Some claimed that this meant he was no longer a Jew, or even a Jewish Christian, but his ancestry and his love and great knowledge of the Old Testament Scriptures negate this idea. It is possible that Paul was linking himself with Galatian traditions, suggesting to these Celts that, although they needed to be disconnected from anti-Christian traditions, it was fine for them to enjoy the good things they had inherited.

This was our thinking, too, when we served as missionaries in Papua New Guinea; many aspects of their culture were quite compatible with Christianity, so why change them? They were part of the people. However, on Dobu Island, the custom of throwing a living baby in the grave with a dead mother, and the practice of cannibalism, were not Christian acts. As the first missionaries dealt with these things and showed a better way, Gods' way, a people who had lived in fear were transformed into a people of love.

GOD'S PLAN FOR PAUL

Paul looked back to the great revelation of his apostolic call: *'But when he, who set me apart before I was born and who called me by his grace, was pleased to reveal his Son to me, in order that I might preach him among the Gentiles, I did not immediately consult with anyone'* (1.15-16). Again, Paul affirmed that his call was straight from God. Even after this astounding experience he did not go to consult with other Apostles in Jerusalem to learn more from them, but went apart to meditate, to think about all that he had learned and experienced from God.

With this new vision it was important to withdraw and spend time thinking about how Jesus Christ and His great sacrifice was the fulfillment of the ancient prophecies in Scripture. By setting this time of quietness aside and waiting on God until the time was right for him to begin his mission, he was being equipped for the experiences that God knew he would have to face in the future.

GOD'S PLAN FOR YOU AND ME

We can also relate Paul's words to our own lives. What an amazing blessing this is for us to think about: God created each one of us uniquely to fulfill the plan that He ordained for us. He chose each of us and set us apart for a special purpose, even before we were born and this includes our family and our environment. Regardless of where we are born, or who our family is, our loving Heavenly Father equips us to fulfill that plan for how we should live and serve Him. However, He has also given us free choice, so it is up to us to choose whether to follow God's plan or to go our own way. Sometimes we may think that we do not have the right gifts to enable us to serve, or we think of some other excuse or reason. Then we remember that *'God doesn't call the equipped, he equips the called.'*

God determines our place in the body of Christ and what we, personally, as individuals, are to do as part of that body. Whether our function is a minor or a major one, we are all important in fitting into just the right place in the jigsaw that is God's scheme. The spiritual gifts that He endows us with are sufficient for us to play our part and they will be consistent with our temperament and the physical and mental abilities that he has given us.

PAUL WAS CALLED BY GOD

Paul wrote: *'He... called me by his grace'* (Galatians 1.15). By His grace, God calls us, too. Just as we must trust God for who we are, we must also trust Him for what we are, whether it's a road-builder, a nurse, a missionary or a parliamentarian, and we must honour that calling and serve in it to the best of our ability.

I wonder how difficult that thought might have been for the Galatians. Their inherited tendencies and culture that encouraged them to plunder and rob would have to end now they had become Christians. That life-style with all its excitement, but also deep uncertainty, had to finish and many of them had no other means of supporting their own lives and their families. Until fairly recently, some had worked as mercenaries for Rome's adversaries, but now they were subject to Roman rule. Like Paul himself, they would have experienced a complete turn around.

This reminds me of a story about a young Christian soldier. One day an officer asked him,
"What is this conversion that you Christians talk about?"
"Sir," the Private replied, "It is like when the Captain calls out, 'Halt!' and then he calls, 'Right about face!' That is what Jesus does. It's like putting our lives under new orders."

Jesus said that this complete change is the same as a rebirth. In fact, He said, *"unless one is born again he cannot see the kingdom of God"* (John 3.3). To some of His listeners, and to many people today, this seems like an absurdity, quite impossible and ridiculous. However, they are Jesus' words and we need to heed them.

Becoming a Christian is not simply making a decision to be good, read the Bible and go to church every Sunday. That is great, but it's only peripheral, skin deep. It needs to come from the depth of the heart, from our whole being. It is not simply changing a life-style, gaining head-knowledge about God and trying to live a better life, it really is a 'Right about face!' The person who is born again, the one who is converted, gives their whole life to Father God, through Jesus. Every part of it is filled with the Holy Spirit and that person is completely changed.

This translation of verse 16, '[God] *was pleased to reveal his Son to me,'* tells us that it pleased God to reveal His Son *to* Paul. However, apparently the Greek actually tells us that Paul intended *in* rather than *to*. That provides us with quite a different meaning. Then we can read it as Paul intended: "God was pleased to reveal His Son *in* me."

Making that personal for me today: "It pleases God to reveal His Son *in* me." Would God really want to reveal His Son in *me*? Let's go back to the Galatians who concerned Paul so much. Before God could truly reveal His Son in their lives, they needed to embrace a whole new way of life. How amazing that God could take such a recalcitrant people and, through Paul and his friends show them how they could make a complete 'About turn' and display the splendour of God in their new lives. It means the same for me; it means the same for all who heed the call-up to serve in His Kingdom. However, we are not conscripted, He gives us the choice to enlist. Making that choice is not just important for our lives now, but for the whole of eternity.

COMMISSIONED BY GOD
There is more: the purpose of this revelation was *'in order that I might preach him among the Gentiles'* (1.16).

On that road to Damascus, God commissioned Paul and gave him a specific mission and that was to proclaim Christ among the Gentiles. The other apostles we have read about were called to serve in different areas, some to the Jews in Jerusalem, others to far-flung places. These Galatians were some of the first people that Paul visited to share the Good News with after his conversion.

PAUL'S MISSION WAS TO THE GENTILES

As we have already seen, Paul's mission from God was to the Gentiles and the Galatians were Gentiles, that is, non-Jews. Probably there were Jews living in the towns that the team visited, so the Celts might have already heard a little about the one true God and the Jewish Scriptures.

Since Paul's visit and the conversion of some of the Galatians, Christian Jews had come and preached among them. They had tried to turn these newly converted Celtic Christians away from Paul and what he had imparted to them. He and Barnabas had taught that when they put their faith in the death and resurrection of Jesus Christ they were saved. These new teachers who had arrived had their background in Judaism and they preached in the Galatian towns that they could never be saved unless they were circumcised (Galatians 5.2–6, 6.12–15) and learned to keep the Law.

When things were straightforward, as proclaimed by Paul and the team in their preaching, they were clear to these Celtic peoples, but when an unknown band of Jewish Christians arrived with their counterclaims, the Galatians were thrown into complete confusion. Their Christianity was so new. Who were they to believe?

Paul reiterated that he *'did not immediately consult with anyone'* (1.16b). He continued to describe his call, telling his readers that after his miraculous call from God he did not consult with anyone else, with no other human person at all. He wanted the Galatians to be quite clear on this point; what he had taught them and preached about while he was with them was straight from God. There was no way that the message could have been adulterated. He did not get it from anyone else and so it was completely correct and what God planned for them to hear.

As Christians today, our mission is the same. Just as Paul shared his story with these Celtic people, so we are called to share our faith story among the people who live wherever God may send us. It might be in our own community at home, or at work, or, like Paul it may be that He has chosen us to be a missionary far from home and way out of our comfort zone.

The important thing is that, like Paul and that young Christian soldier, we are obedient to Jesus, our Captain, and follow His orders.

To Think About or Discuss

1. Have you ever told your faith story? How did you feel? Did your audience listen? What were their comments?

2. Discuss the process of conversion in the light of Jesus' statement that we must be born again. Do you know anyone who has experienced a startling conversion? How did you become a Christian?

3. What scriptures have you learnt by heart? Do you still remember those passages?

≈6≈

PAUL'S RETREAT AND PREPARATION
CHAPTER 1. 17 - 24

After this amazing life-changing experience, the things that mattered to Paul were his relationship with God and his mission from God, and those only.

1 *[17]nor did I go up to Jerusalem to those who were apostles before me, but I went away into Arabia, and returned again to Damascus.*
[18]Then after three years I went up to Jerusalem to visit Cephas and remained with him fifteen days; [19]but I saw none of the apostles except James the Lord's brother. [20](In what I am writing to you, before God, I do not lie!) [21]Then I went into the regions of Syria and Cilicia. [22]And I was still unknown in person to the churches of Judea that are in Christ. [23]They only were hearing it said, 'He who used to persecute us is now preaching the faith he once tried to destroy.' [24]And they glorified God because of me.

PAUL RECUPERATED IN DAMASCUS

God's tremendous revelation of Jesus Christ was such a dazzling experience that Paul was left blind for a time and his travelling companions *'led him by the hand'* (Acts 9.8) as they continued on to Damascus (*see* pp. 35-36).

After his sight had been restored, Paul spent a short time with some disciples in Damascus, probably receiving further teaching from them. Now he needed more time to think about his dramatic conversion, to readjust his thoughts, his life-style, and his attitude to almost everything in his life that had gone on before.

PAUL'S RETREAT
He set out from the walled oasis city of Damascus on a journey that led across the desert to Arabia. At that time Roman Arabia included much of modern Saudi Arabia, Jordan, and southern Syria. We are not told how far he travelled or who travelled with him, but it was most likely that he did not travel alone, for safety's sake.

This time of retreat was so necessary. Possibly at times Paul, with all his youthful energy and enthusiasm, was longing to begin his mission, but he needed a time of withdrawal and preparation.

Times of retreat, of waiting on God, of drawing apart are important for us, too. If we are to be good 'Ambassadors for Christ' we first need to take time and be prepared. A period of retreat into a safe sanctuary or Bible College where we can study God's word may cause us to feel as if we are marking time when we have made a commitment and are anxious to begin the work God has called us to do. But God knows that this time of preparation of our hearts and minds is important if we are to understand the best way to share the good news to different people groups who have a world-view and culture very different from our own.

BACK IN DAMASCUS
After his time of withdrawal, Paul journeyed back from Arabia and returned to Damascus. Then he began to preach the wonderful good news about Jesus in the synagogues, possibly to the very Jews who had supported his persecution of the Christians who followed 'The Way.'

The Jews were astonished at this new message. Perhaps Paul was a little tentative with his preaching at first, as we are told in Acts (9.22), he '*increased... in strength.*' This increased strength was in his preaching of the message that Jesus was indeed the Christ and it may have been the strengthening of his body also. He would need physical strength for his next step in God's plan.

This new message was not what the Jews wanted to hear and they began to plot, making plans to kill Paul. They did not see it as good news at all! They wanted to see this new 'sect' completely eradicated. Paul, or some of his friends and supporters, heard about the plot. He found that the gates to Damascus were being watched in case he tried to escape. But escape he did! He now had his own group of disciples, and they let him down over the city wall in a basket in the dead of night. We're not told if he had any companions in the venture, but he may have, for protection.

PAUL WENT TO JERUSALEM

We do not know how long Paul spent in Arabia before returning to Damascus, but he wrote: *'after three years I went up to Jerusalem to visit Cephas and remained with him fifteen days;* [19]*but I saw none of the other apostles except James the Lord's brother.* [20]*(In what I am writing to you, before God, I do not lie!)'* (1.18-20).

Paul travelled to Jerusalem. The plot to kill him was the catalyst that God needed to urge Paul that it was time to move on. God had many plans for Paul. Eventually he was to become one of the most important people in the history of Christianity, writing many letters and travelling vast distances as he shared his faith, especially with Gentiles. The Celts, with their long history of wandering around Europe, would easily relate to Paul's tales of his travels.

It is thought that Paul was converted around A.D. 33. This would date his visit to Jerusalem at about A.D. 36, so this may be the visit described in Acts 9.26-29. In this account we find that when he arrived the disciples there were afraid that he had come to persecute them. His reputation had gone before him and they wanted nothing to do with him. What was he plotting now? Why was he pretending to be a disciple of Jesus when they knew he had worked diligently to exterminate them? The other apostles would not see him. However, Barnabas knew about Paul's conversion and that he was genuine, so he took him to visit Cephas (1.18).[15] There has been some confusion as to whether Paul referred to Peter, or if there was another apostle called Cephas. It is interesting to read even further about this dilemma.[16]

BARNABAS

Barnabas,[17] as we find in Acts 4.36, was actually a Jew from Cyprus named Joseph, and a descendant of the Jewish priestly tribe of Levi. He had become a Christian and a member of the church in Jerusalem. The Apostles had renamed him Barnabas, possibly at his baptism.

The Book of Leviticus is concerned with the priesthood, the worship of God and the priests' responsibility to teach God's people about the need for holiness. God is so holy

---

[15] **Cephas and Peter:** There is some confusion about this name: whether it was the Apostle Peter, or if there was another who was called Cephas. He mentions this name again in 2.9 and earlier in that same sentence (2.8) he mentions Peter, so it is possible that Cephas and Peter were two separate people, although some later theologians are unsure. According to Clement of Alexandria, Simon, son of John, whom Jesus nicknamed Peter (meaning stone or rock in Greek), was one of the original twelve disciples, while Cephas (meaning a rock in Aramaic) was one of the Seventy Apostles.

[16] Eusebius wrote a history of Christianity that covered the time of the disciples until about 325 A.D. He recorded Clement of Alexandria as saying that it was Cephas of the Seventy who was condemned by Paul for refusing to eat with the Gentiles (*see* Galatians 2.11-12). As Clement had been born about 160 A.D., not much more than a hundred years after Paul's letter to the Galatians, this information may have been handed down by word of mouth. It could be a little like 'James the Lord's brother,' who was usually referred to with that appellation to differentiate him from the other James.

[17] Barnabas: 'son of encouragement'

that it's impossible for Him to dwell with unholy people. It was His desire that all Israel would be holy so *'all the families of the earth shall be blessed'* (Genesis 12.3).

Barnabas was a great supporter and encourager of Paul and because of his Levite background and Paul's studies of the Jewish Law they probably had much in common to share on their travels. After the long walk on dusty roads where danger lurked, Barnabas took him to meet Cephas, and Paul *'stayed with him fifteen days'* (1.18). Over this fortnight, they had many deep discussions, during which Paul told the story of his conversion and other experiences in Damascus (1.18).

Paul wrote that the only other Apostle he met in Jerusalem was James, the brother of Jesus (1.19). This suggests that James was now counted among the Apostles although he, too, was not one of the original twelve. Later when he wrote to the Corinthians (1 Cor. 9.4-5) Paul mentioned the believing wives of the other Apostles, of Cephas and the brothers of the Lord. It appears that all the other Apostles were married and only Paul and Barnabas were celibate. James was head of the church in Jerusalem.

PREACHING BOLDLY

Paul was accepted by Cephas and James, and then attempted to share his faith in Jerusalem, *'preaching boldly in the name of the Lord'* (Acts 9.28) and debating with the Jews there, as they loved to do (Acts 9.29). However, they became angry and soon his life was in danger again. Once more, some of the Christians heard of the Jews' plots and secretly escorted Paul safely to Caesarea. He wrote, *'Then I went into the regions of Syria and Cilicia'* (1.21). He returned to his home in Tarsus in the province of Cilicia

That term, *'preaching boldly'* is a great example for Christians today. There are so many events, celebrations, and even bills that are presented in parliament, that are abhorrent for Christians, and they seem to occur frequently in our nations and communities. The subjects in question can be in complete contrast to what the Scriptures teach us, but often we are tempted to pussyfoot around these topics instead of speaking out against them. First, we need to pray and be sure that what we are contemplating is within God's will for us. Then let us be bold like Paul in our preaching, talking, and even in speaking out to our members of parliament to let them know how we feel and think.

So at this time Paul stayed away, and remained unknown except by hearsay among the Christian Jewish churches in Jerusalem and its surroundings:
'and I was still unknown in person to the churches of Judea that are in Christ. ^{23} They were only hearing it said, "He who used to persecute us is now preaching the faith he once tried to destroy"' (1.22-23).

But this knowledge was enough. The Christians believed what they heard and gave God the glory for this wonderful transformation in Paul. He wrote: *'And they glorified God because of me'* (1.24).

To Think About or Discuss

1. Discuss waiting on God and/ or going on a retreat. How did you deal with it? How did it affect your relationship with God?

2. Have you, or someone you know, ever been in a dangerous situation while serving God? What happened?

3. What do you do when you find out about a situation in the nation or the community that you know is contrary to the Word of God? Would you do anything?

≈7≈

PAUL'S ACCEPTANCE
CHAPTER 2. 1 - 10

Before we begin this section, it is interesting to note that the Scriptures Paul used were not divided into chapters and verses, although the Hebrew Bible did by then have a marker for the ending of a paragraph. Some Books were divided into sections so that they could be read aloud in weekly worship over the course of a set period, such as a year, or even three years as we still do with our Lectionary in many Christian denominations and churches.

After the time of Jesus, different divisions were made in the Scriptures in a number of countries, but there are still translations available that do not have these divisions, so that the Bible may be read as literature. However, among others, Bishop Stephen Langton, Archbishop of Canterbury in the 1200s developed a system of divisions into chapters and verses for ease of reference and study and this was eventually adopted almost universally.

In Chapter Two (1.10), Paul testified that the message he taught had been acknowledged and approved by the other leading apostles when he later visited Jerusalem and had discussions with them.

2 *[1]Then after fourteen years I went up again to Jerusalem with Barnabas taking Titus along with me. [2]I went up because of a revelation and set before them (though privately before those who seemed to be influential) the gospel that I proclaim among the Gentiles, in order to make sure I was not running, or had not run, in vain. [3]But even Titus, who was with me, was not forced to be circumcised, though he was a Greek. [4]Yet because of false brothers secretly brought in, who slipped in to spy out our* *freedom that we have in Christ Jesus, so that they might bring us to slavery –* ^{5}*we did not yield to them in submission even for a moment, so that the truth of the gospel might be preserved for you.* ^{6}*And from those who seemed to be influential (what they were makes no difference to me; God shows no partiality) –* ^{7}*Those, I say, who seemed influential added nothing to me. When they saw that I had been entrusted with the gospel to the uncircumcised, just as Peter had been entrusted with the gospel to the circumcised* ^{8}*(for he who worked through Peter through his apostolic ministry to the circumcised worked also through me for mine to the Gentiles),* ^{9}*and when James and Cephas and John, who seemed to be pillars, perceived the grace that was given to me, they gave the right hand of fellowship to Barnabas and me, that we should go to the Gentiles and they to the circumcised.* ^{10}*Only they asked us to remember the poor, the very thing I was eager to do.*

Paul had studied the Old Testament Law in depth with some of the best teachers of his time. Sometimes he is referred to as 'Paul the lawyer;' he knew what he was speaking and writing about. He had been trained by the best of the times to present a case with passion and power and he utilized that training to the best of his ability.

PAUL RETURNED TO JERUSALEM
Paul, with Barnabas[18] and Titus, returned to Jerusalem '*after fourteen years*' (2.1). This length of time could refer to an additional fourteen years after the three years mentioned in 1.18. The fourteen years could also start from Paul's conversion, and include the three. The latter seems

---

[18] Barnabas was a faithful fellow worker with Paul. His saint's day is 11th June and his symbol a rake as this is the time of the hay harvest. During his ministry he supported Paul in the harvest of people for God.

slightly more probable as this would place their visit at around A.D. 47. So it is most likely that for about the next eight years Paul remained in Syria and Cilicia, ministering to the people there. His ministry was not 'all smooth sailing' as at times he met with opposition and was attacked both verbally and bodily, as he was certainly not one to mince words.

After this, Paul returned to Jerusalem. This visit probably corresponds to Acts 11 29-30, which described a devastating famine in Judea. Christians who were not affected were requested to send relief and Paul travelled there in response to a revelation (2.2). God showed him the need and he and his co-workers collected money and took it to Jerusalem to save the poor Christians there from starvation.

As was customary in those days, for safety they may have shared the money they had collected. They would then have sewn it into their robes and other clothing in case they met any marauding teams of bandits that frequented the hills beside the road on their journey.

It was thought among both Romans and Jews that a trade should be learned so that, if needed, those going on to further study could support themselves later. Paul's home was in Tarsus, a centre for the manufacture of linen fabric, one of the materials from which tents were made, so it was ideal for Paul. The apprenticeship usually began when the boy was about thirteen years of age and when it was concluded the person graduating was presented with a set of the tools of his trade.

Paul had learned the skills of tent making and the awls and thimbles were small and easy for him to carry on his travels. He would have been handy with the needle for secreting the offering of the people in this way and he was also able to support himself in many places where he stopped on his long missionary travels.

THE LEADERS' CONFERENCE

After labouring for fourteen years to take the Good News to the Gentiles, Paul had the opportunity to confirm that what he had been preaching was in accordance with the stance of some of the Apostles who had been with Jesus and had learned the Gospel first-hand from Him. The leaders at the meeting probably included James, Peter and John (2.9). He wrote, *'I laid before them (though only in a private meeting with the acknowledged leaders) the gospel that I proclaim among the Gentiles, in order to make sure that I was not running, or had not run, in vain'* (2.2). These leaders were the most influential apostles, but Paul was not intimidated by their standing; all are equal before God. 'Run' is such a good word for Paul, as he appeared to be so driven to spread the gospel that he often seemed to be on the run.

The Jerusalem apostles agreed that Titus,[19] a Greek and therefore a Gentile, *'was not forced to be circumcised'* (Galatians 2.3). From this Paul concluded that the church leaders agreed that no Gentile needed circumcision. However, some whose mission was to the Jews, and the 'false believers' who had infiltrated the meeting, continued to disagree, but Paul's group *'did not yield to them even for*

---

[19] Paul had converted Titus and consistently refused his circumcision; as a Gentile he was free from obeying Jewish Law. Paul commissioned Titus to minister to the Gentiles and was mentioned in several Letters. According to tradition, Paul later consecrated Titus to serve as Bishop on the island of Crete. As Paul requested, he contributed to church organization by appointing leaders, or 'elders' in every city (*'The Letter of Paul to Titus'*). When old, Titus remained in Crete, so he must have loved the people, although they had been renowned as inveterate liars before he took the Gospel there and taught about Christians maintaining *'upright, holy, and disciplined'* (Titus 1. 8) lives. Titus died, aged about ninety-five, in the city of Candia (now Heraklion), and his skull is in the Church of St. Titus there.

a moment, so that the truth of the gospel might be preserved' (2.5).

We can imagine that some of the discussion was quite heated, but Paul and his party stood firmly for the truth and did not waver as the discussion continued. He describes this confrontation in his letter, as he wanted the Galatians to understand that what he had taught them was the true gospel and that it related to them.

ALL ARE EQUAL BEFORE GOD

Paul emphasized that the apostles had equal standing in God's sight. He was not inferior to any of the others: *'from those who seemed to be influential (what they were makes no difference to me; God shows no partiality)'* (Galatians 2.6). He had been assigned by Jesus Himself to evangelize the uncircumcised, the Gentiles, while Cephas was sent to minister to the circumcised, the Jews. Here, Paul is implying that the Galatians should not consider themselves inferior to any other Christian believers.

Although they were fellow Christians and leaders on an equal footing, Paul and his group were called by God to share the Gospel with different communities that represented different cultures:
[7]*'when they saw that I had been entrusted with the gospel for the uncircumcised, just as Peter had been entrusted with the gospel to the circumcised* [8]*(for he who worked through Peter for his apostolic ministry to the circumcised worked also through me for mine to the Gentiles).'* The culture and world-view of the people they worked with were different and these were to be respected when they did not clash with the Christian standpoint.

This remains so for missionaries today. In the past, missionaries sometimes made the mistake of expecting new converts to take on all the trappings of Western culture, and this caused problems, as well as adverse criticism from non-Christians in the western world. Of course, like the Cretans, there were many aspects of their lives and attitudes that needed to change, especially the Cretans' culture of lying, if they were to live as Christians. However, there was no need to change anything in their culture that was not contrary to living *'upright, holy and disciplined*,' Christ-centred lives, including their world-view and way of life.

PILLARS OF THE CHURCH
Paul recognized that some church leaders had greater strength of leadership than others, and had been endowed with a variety of 'fruit of the Spirit' and that God used these in different ways. He continued: *'when James and Cephas and John, who seemed to be pillars, perceived the grace that was given to me, they gave the right hand of fellowship to Barnabas and me that we should go to the Gentiles and they to the circumcised'* (Galatians 2.9).

Cephas, James and John were leaders in the early church and Paul confirmed this when he wrote that they were acknowledged as pillars. It is significant that these apostles gave the right hand of fellowship to Barnabas and Paul. They were welcomed as part of the inner group of leaders, but their mission was different. This showed Paul that they approved of the gospel he preached and recognized his ministry to the Gentiles (2.9). At this juncture, Paul did not mention Titus, although from the earlier part of his letter it appears that he had remained with Paul and Barnabas. Perhaps Titus was omitted because of his background; he was a Gentile, so it was logical that his mission was to the Gentiles, whereas Paul and Barnabas's background was Jewish.

Paul's mention of James, Cephas and John as 'pillars' may have influenced some 'saints,' centuries later, to withdraw from the world and live as hermits on the top of pillars,

rather than in caves. They were called Pillar Saints, or 'Stylites.' The best known were:
- **Simeon the Stylite** of Syria. He spent 37 years on different pillars; the highest was 66 feet high. He died in 460, aged 72.

- **Daniel the Stylite** of Constantinople. He lived for 33 years on a pillar and was often buffeted by storms. He died in 494.

Such unusual withdrawal from the accepted mode of living may have given the Stylites opportunities for meditation and prayer, but, apart from the spectacle and the danger of such activities, I wonder how much it advanced the spread of the Gospel.

AID FOR THE POOR

The other apostles that Paul had discussions with did have a request to make of the little team of visitors. *'They asked us to remember the poor, the very thing that I was eager to do'* (2.10).

This probably referred mainly to poor[20] Jewish Christians who were living in Jerusalem. As we saw, there had been a famine in Judea and these brothers and sisters were suffering because of it. Paul did not mention this again in his *'Letter of Paul to the Galatians'* but there is a later reference to it in his *'Letter of Paul to the Romans'* (15.25-26). Here we find that Paul led an effort to aid them.

---

[20] There are around 207 references in the Bible to the poor, many of them in the Old Testament. In both Testaments, it is considered a good thing to help the poor. One example was Job. In a test Satan deprived Job of everything he owned, but he steadfastly refused to sacrifice his principles and never blamed God for his suffering and poverty.

Paul was 'eager' to help and his enthusiasm is a great example for us. There are so many worthy causes that sometimes we almost reach burn out. We see many bad things happening in our own country and overseas and become inured to their plight. The vastness of the needs of others is so much that we turn a blind eye, feeling that anything we can offer is too small. But every little can help and Paul's eagerness is typical of the man. He did not have much, but he was able to encourage others to give – and to give with a willing heart.

To Think About or Discuss

1. If you continued with further study courses after leaving school, how were you supported during that time? How did you us that skill used later, if at all?

2. Discuss the variety of skills that missionaries today can use to reach different people groups? How are they equipped?

3. In what ways does your church support people in need? Do you know about all the agencies of your church that do this?

≈8≈

PAUL CONDEMNED HYPOCRISY
CHAPTER 2. 11 - 14

2 [11] But when Cephas came to Antioch, I opposed him to his face, because he stood condemned. [12] For before certain men came from James, he was eating with the Gentiles, but when they came he drew back and separated himself fearing the circumcision party. [13] And the rest of the Jews acted hypocritically along with him, so that even Barnabas was led astray by their hypocrisy. [14] But when I saw that their conduct was not in step with the truth of the gospel, I said to Cephas before them all, "If you, though a Jew, live like a Gentile and not like a Jew, how can you force the Gentiles to live like Jews?"

We have found (2.1-10) that Paul did not aim to be a people pleaser. His goal was to please God and do His will. Now, to prove his point, he used a situation where he confronted Cephas when they were in Antioch and even opposed him *'to his face'* (2.11). Paul's mission was to the Gentiles, which included these Celts that he had evangelized and then followed that by setting up house churches. He urgently longed for the Galatians and other Gentiles to understand that they were not inferior to the Jewish Christians.

JEWISH FOOD LAWS

The situation appears to be that when Cephas was visiting the church in Antioch and, when invited, he ate with the Galatian Christians. Then some Jewish Christians arrived from the Jerusalem church led by James. They continued to eat separately and follow the kosher food laws. Paul is not criticizing this; it was their cultural heritage. He opposed Cephas because he was being hypocritical. Cephas accepted this reprimand, acknowledging Paul as Leader.

When Cephas first arrived, he ate whatever he was offered by the Gentile Christians, and he ate with them, although this broke with Jewish tradition. The circumcision group required that Jewish Christians should continue to obey the Mosaic covenant laws about food and the observance of special days. When the other Jewish Christians arrived, Cephas sat apart with them, abandoning the Galatians' hospitality and only eating kosher food. Perhaps he did not realize that his example could make the Gentile Christians feel like second-class Christians. Barnabas was also led astray in this way and Paul reprimanded him, too, for his hypocrisy.

From this event we learn that early notions about how Christians should relate to the Law of Moses suggested that Jewish Christians could continue to observe the traditions of the Mosaic code,[21] but it was acceptable for Gentile believers not to observe its stipulations. They were under the New Covenant and the Law was not their way of salvation. Paul was concerned that Jewish traditions should not be imposed on other ethnic groups who were not Jews.

Paul saw the actions of Cephas and Barnabas as hypocrisy and inconsistent. He pointed out publicly that, although they had their Jewish heritage, now they were Christians they were free from those laws. They had not observed the food laws until the circumcision party criticized them. Now Cephas, quite illogically, was expecting Gentile Christians to adhere to Jewish kosher food laws, if he were to eat with them. It was not part of their culture and did not make sense. Paul was strong enough to point this out in no uncertain terms.

---

[21] 'Mosaic' here refers to the laws that God gave Moses. It is not to be confused with the same word that is used in the term, 'mosaic work.' 'Mosaic work' is connected with the Muses and the tessellated floors that were first used in the heathen grottoes that were consecrated to the Muses.

Are we never guilty of being hypocrites? To be a hypocrite means that we claim to have higher moral standards than actually show in the way we live and act. I have a feeling we do this far more than we would like to admit.

JESUS IS OUR EXAMPLE

We know the standards that Jesus set by His example, and would like to emulate them, but we do not always do so.

There's a story about King Henry VIII: In 1538, he issued a decree to all the churches in England commanding that before Easter the following year every church was to possess a large copy of the Bible in English, instead of the current ones in Latin, and that these Bibles were to be available for all the people to read, not just the clergy. Both clergy and parishioners were to contribute to its purchase. He saw it as the living Word of God and stated that no one was to be prevented from reading it, but should be encouraged to do so.

This one, momentous act of opened up the Bible for all people who could read or hear the Word in their own language, was a great innovation. It encouraged ordinary people to find out more about God's Word, to understand it better and to engrave it in their hearts and lives. This bold move led many to believe and be saved. The King's ideals and moral standards were high, but if we look at some facets of his own life, he did not always maintain these standards. We may be like that, too. We should remain alert to our own shortcomings and, with God's help try and avoid being hypocrites.

Returning to verse 14, we find that here it has been translated as meaning *'live like a Gentile/ live like a Jew,'* Other versions give 'walk' instead of live. The translation as 'live' probably fits with Paul's intention here, as 'walk' when it is used as a reference to moral conduct was a Jewish concept that the Jews would have known well, but it may not have been so easily understood by these Celtic converts from the pagan world. Paul's intention in the letter is to eradicate misunderstandings and heal rifts among these new Christians so that they could conduct their lives in a way that shows love for each other and that pleases God. We now live under the truth of the gospel, in love for one another.

FREE, BUT WITH SENSITIVITY

We need to be aware of cultural traditions. As Christians, we are free to eat whatever is offered, but we need to be sensitive to other traditions, and our own ethnicity may cause us problems, too.

As a practical illustration, there was an occasion when my husband, Andrew, needed to deal with this. When we were serving as missionaries in Papua New Guinea we learned to dearly love our brothers and sisters there. We mostly ate the kind of food that we were used to, but were happy to try anything new, especially if it was fresh, as most western food came in packets and tins, apart from what we grew in our garden. If we visited in the villages, we ate what was offered. Apparently this became known and was appreciated, as some people of other cultures refused to try local food.

Once, while I remained at home on the 'Station' with the children, Andrew, as Mission Education Officer, went off in a boat with some local medical orderlies who were to visit villages in some remote islands. Andrew was going to inspect the schools. At one village he was offered hospitality in the Head Teacher's house and stayed there for the night. Our liking for sharing local food had gone before him. For the evening meal he was given a whole possum (skinned and cooked), including the head. It was an honour, but he found it a little difficult, as the flesh was softer than our usual meats. He did his best, but could not finish, relieved when the plate was removed. The next morning he was presented with the remains for his breakfast! He never forgot that experience. I wonder if how he felt was a little like the Jews felt when they were expected to refrain from obeying the Jewish kosher food laws.

However, choosing to share with Christian brothers and sisters is different from compelling them to follow cultural rules that have nothing to do with Christian morality. When we are working overseas among other cultures, or even welcoming people of other ethnic groups to our church, it is important that we define for ourselves the difference between Christianity and culture and do not try and impose our own ways where it is not necessary.

To Think About or Discuss

1. How do we feel when we are reprimanded? To what extent should we accept criticism when we think that we have done our best in the situation?

2. In the Scriptures, what other evidence can you find of hypocrisy similar to the actions of Cephas and Barnabas? Have you ever found yourself in a difficult situation because of cultural differences? What would you have done if you had been Andrew?

3. Discuss the fact that we should now live under the truth of the gospel, showing our love for each other and for our neighbour. Would our neighbour be able to tell from the way that we live that Jesus is our model and we are trying to follow Him?

≈9≈

THE LAW OR FAITH
CHAPTER 2. 15 - 21

2 [15] *We ourselves are Jews by birth and not Gentile sinners;* [16] *yet we know that a person is justified not by the works of the law but through faith in Jesus Christ, so we also have believed in Christ Jesus, in order to be justified by faith in Christ and not by works of the law, because by works of the law no one will be justified.* [17] *But if, in our endeavour to be justified in Christ, we too were found to be sinners, is Christ then a servant of sin? Certainly not!* [18] *For if I rebuild what I tore down, I prove myself to be a transgressor.* [19] *For through the law I died to the law, so that I might live to God.* [20] *I have been crucified with Christ. It is no longer I who live, but Christ who lives in me. And the life I now live in the flesh I live by faith in the Son of God, who loved me and gave himself for me* [21] *I do not nullify the grace of God; for if righteousness were through the law, then Christ died for no purpose.*

This is a key passage in Paul's letter. It is his explanation of justification. In the Bible, this word has a special meaning; we can only be justified before God by being freed of our sins and made righteous through Jesus.

1. JUSTIFICATION IS BY FAITH

Can we be made righteous before God by obeying the Law? The Law only attracts our attention to the fact that it must be kept and so the spotlight is on sin and the consequences if we break it. The Law is not, and could never be the way to justification. That is only achieved through our faith in Jesus Christ. In verses 15-16, Paul stressed the fallacy of the notion that, by being born a Jew, he was justified, while the Gentiles, by being born outside the law, remained sinners and counted as unjustified.

In the same way, we cannot claim to be righteous because we were born into a Christian family, nor even because of our attendance at worship, or the work we do for the church. We are all sinners and the only way we can be justified is through our faith in Jesus Christ.

2. JEWS MUST BE JUSTIFIED BY FAITH

Paul pointed out that, although he and the others in the mission team had been born Jews, and had been reared to learn and obey the Law, that is not the way of justification; the only way to be right with God is through faith in Jesus Christ. Paul and the team were Jews by birth and they understood Jewish customs and ways of thinking, so when they taught Jews about Jesus, they lived under the law like Jews in order to win them for Christ, but when they lived with the Galatians, they lived as Gentiles, so he could understand their ways and so win them for Christ.

Paul wrote that *'no one will be justified by the works of the law'* (2.16). The visiting Christian Jews were misguided in their evangelism as they tried to persuade the Gentile Galatians that they needed to practice circumcision and outward ceremonies and obedience to the Mosaic Law and that the whole Old Testament law was necessary in order to be right with God; that was the way of justification (*see also* Galatians 4.17 and 6.12-13) and how a person is counted righteous before God. But Paul explained that only through faith in Christ could one be right with God. Paul was adamant about this; it was vital. The word *'justified'* is mentioned three times in verse 16 and again in verse 17. Justification is by faith alone. Paul's words are timeless and true. We are not justified and counted as righteous by our own merit, but only through faith in Jesus Christ.

THE ESSENCE OF THE LAW

The tenet held by the Jewish Christians was that if people obeyed every one of God's perfect moral standards as set out in Old Testament Law, they could be justified by their own merits. There are 613 laws in the Torah. Three hundred and sixty-five lay down instructions on what people are to avoid doing and the remaining 248 state what the people of God are to do. These laws were to be strictly observed. In fact, one law said that not one of them was to be deleted. No wonder that Paul, when he was Saul had to spend so long studying them! Jesus, on the other hand, reduced the 613 laws down to their very essence: two basic laws that we should love God with all our might and love our neighbour as ourselves.

Paul said it is impossible for anyone to obey the whole of the Law, so no one can be justified by his own merits (*see* Romans 1-2). Doing the 'works of the law' can never lead to any person being justified by God through their own efforts; we can only be justified before God through belief. *'We also have believed in Christ Jesus, in order to be justified by faith in Christ'* (2.16) means that justification can only be the result of faith. It is faith alone! No human effort or good work can be added as a basis for justification (*see* Acts 13.39, Galatians 3.10-14).

Paul wrote, *'if I rebuild what I tore down, I prove myself to be a transgressor'* (2.18). He could not turn the clock back and undo what he did before becoming a Christian. Even if he made reparation, he remained a sinner. Nor can we go back and right past wrongs; only through our faith in Jesus can our Heavenly Father forgive us. Ironically, the person who is most clearly seen to be a sinner is not the one outside the Law, the Gentile, but the one under the Law.

The Law taught Paul that he could not be saved by works, as he explained: *'For through the law I died to the law'* (2.19a). But Paul died to the Law: he no longer tried to gain justification by obedience to it. He knew the Law, but he was no longer under it; his new life was a complete contrast to his old life under the Law. He was now under the lordship of Christ and nothing could be more different; he was made alive in Christ. Why? He wrote: *'So that I might live to God'* (2.19b). That is life abundant. Paul gained God's acceptance through justification in Christ. He had amazing new freedom to live totally devoted to God.

3. THROUGH FAITH CHRIST LIVES IN US

We have that freedom, too. Christ loves us and gave His life for each of us as *individuals*. *'I have been crucified with Christ. It is no longer I who live, but it is Christ who lives in me.* (2.20a). This is a well-loved verse in both word and song; it has such a depth of meaning. When I become a Christian, 'I' am no longer the centre of my universe. It is Christ living in me. *Everything* is Christ centred.

Remember that Jesus did not only say *'Abide in me,'* but He also said, *'I in you'* (John 15.4). The Epistles speak not only of us living in Christ, but also of Christ living in us. This is one of the greatest mysteries of His redeeming love.

As we maintain our place in Christ day by day, God waits to reveal Christ in us in such a way that He is formed in us. His mind, character and likeness take on substance and form in us, so that we can say, *'it is Christ who lives in me'* (2.20). Jesus Christ, the Holy One of Israel, actually comes and lives in me! Impossible! How can we make that happen? We cannot. Nothing we can do could ever bring this about. We are completely helpless, apart from the fact that we can wait on God in prayer. When we wait on Him in faith, our minds and thoughts concentrate more and more on Him until Christ is revealed in us. As we wait on God and abide in Him, then He will come and abide in us. It is a daily work – and a daily joy.

When Paul wrote *'it is no longer I who live'* (2.20), he did not mean that he no longer had a personality of his own. It meant that he no longer had control of his own life, he had handed it over to God, *'it is Christ who lives'* in him. As Paul trusted Jesus Christ every step of the way, Jesus worked in and through him in all that he did, *'the life I now live in the flesh I live by faith in the Son of God, who loved me and gave himself for me'* (2.20).

It is the same for us: Christ who lives in us now directs and empowers all that we do when we trust in Christ and He abides in us. Through Christ, the life we now live in the flesh we live by faith in Him. He loves me and gave himself for me: the crucifixion shows us Christ's love for each of us as individuals.

The Holy Spirit will never mislead us about the Father's will. In order that we do not miss the purpose God has for us, He has given His Spirit to guide us according to His will. In Jesus, we have the picture of a perfect love relationship with the Father. Jesus, our supreme example, consistently lived out that relationship. We are a long way from that, but Christ is present in us to help us to know and do God's will. We need to adjust our lives to God and faithfully live out that relationship with absolute dependence on Him. He will never fail to draw us into the middle of His purpose and enable us to do it, as He did for people throughout Scripture.

CHRIST'S FAITH, MY FAITH

The faith by which Jesus Christ lived, His faith in God and His Kingdom, is expressed in the gospel He preached; the good news that the kingdom rule of God is available to humankind here and now. His followers did not have this faith within themselves, and for quite along time they regarded it only as His faith, not theirs. Even after they came to faith in Him they did not share His deep faith. During the storm on Galilee, Jesus asked, 'Why are you so afraid? Have you still no faith' (Mark 4.37-41)?

The disciples' faith had obviously grown. They called upon Jesus, trusting Him to save them. But they did not have His great faith in God. It was because they did not have His faith that He spoke of how little faith they had. Sometimes we Christians demonstrate that the notions of faith and love for Christ leave Christ outside the personality of the believer. Could some of the modern translations of the Bible be influenced by the need to turn our weak efforts into the norms of faith? These are exterior notions and they cannot provide the deep abiding that causes us, the branches, to bring forth much fruit. Only by our abiding as branches can we be reconciled to God through the death of his Son. God's life in us, Jesus' thoughts, His faith, and His love, are then implanted, grafted into us through His Holy Spirit and Christ's faith becomes our faith.

4. JUSTIFICATION AND GOD'S GRACE

Christ's death would have been pointless if we could achieve righteousness through the Law. Then we could earn justification by our obedience to it, but we can never do this. Sin is such a serious matter before our holy God that only the atoning death of His Son can deal with the problem. Salvation can never come through the Law, only through Christ crucified and the grace of God.

Paul did *'not nullify the grace of God; for if righteousness were through the law, then Christ died for no purpose'* (2.21). If we could obtain justification by doing good works in obedience to the Law, then Jesus' crucifixion would have been pointless. God does not do unnecessary things. The Law of faith through Jesus, the *'law of Christ'* (Galatians 6.2) has replaced the Law of Moses.

5. CHOOSE FAITH

Paul laid it on the line for the Galatians. He insisted that they make the most momentous decision of their lives: choose to believe these preachers and follow the Law or have faith in God through the death and resurrection of Jesus Christ. We, too, must make that choice. It has been the same for each person for over two thousand years.

Faith is the key! Faith is complete trust, having total confidence in the One who loved us so much that He gave His sinless life as a sacrifice for our sinful lives. The Law can be a guide, but it can only make us aware of how far we fall short; through it we can never achieve justification before our Almighty Father.

Faith is not a 'maybe,' half-hearted state of mind; it goes to the very core of our being. The true depth of faith has been shown to us again and again through the characters and the events they faced as told in the Bible, right from the beginning of the Old Testament.

Faith is *complete* trust. Remember the story of Noah and the Ark? God gave Noah specific instructions for the construction of the ark: the type of wood, the exact measurements and the placement of the door (Genesis 6.14-16). However, when we explore these instructions further, some important details are conspicuous by their absence. Have you noticed that God omitted any specifications for a sail, a steering wheel or a rudder? Whoever heard of anyone building a ship without these essentials? Yet, Noah followed God's instructions. He had faith that God knew exactly what He was planning.

To Think About or Discuss
1. Why is justification through belief in Jesus important?

2. What importance does the Law have for the Christian today?

3. Why do we need, as each individual person to put our faith in Jesus Christ?

≈10≈

THE HOLY SPIRIT: THE WAY TO SALVATION
CHAPTER 3. 1 - 5

3 ¹O foolish Galatians! Who has bewitched you? It was before your eyes that Jesus Christ was publicly portrayed as crucified! ²Let me ask you only this: Did you receive the Spirit by works of the law or by hearing with faith? ³Are you so foolish? Having begun by the Spirit, are you now being perfected by the flesh? ⁴Did you suffer so many things in vain? – if indeed it was in vain. ⁵Does he who supplies the Spirit to you and works miracles among you do so by the works of the law, or by hearing with faith?

Paul was upset by the Galatians' fickleness. Twice he called them foolish for listening to teachers who led them astray. Their message must be resisted or they would lose the true way to salvation. He was so disappointed that they listened to the preaching that he reminded them again of how they first came to know Christ. The theme that Paul introduced here was an alarm warning, a wake up call. It began in Chapter 3.1 and continued to the end of Chapter 4. He put the case strongly to the Galatians that they must choose between obeying a Law of rituals, or by hearing the message of the Gospel and believing it. He told them to remember all he had taught them, that faith brings righteousness; the Holy Spirit is the true way of salvation.

THE WORK OF THE HOLY SPIRIT
Paul again reminded these Celts that when he was with them he taught Christ crucified, and they believed. How could they have been so easily deceived and led astray? Salvation in Christ is by faith, not by works. Paul wrote that they had learned this through the Holy Spirit. They had received the Holy Spirit in their lives but were now allowing themselves to be dragged down. The new

teaching of the Christian Jews had caused these Celts to regress to their former, unbelieving way of life and thought. He reminded them that salvation could only ever be through faith in Christ; through Him alone both Jews and Gentiles could have complete salvation.

Paul asked *'Who has bewitched you'?* (3.1a), who cast a spell over you? When he asked this, he was referring to their former pagan magic practices. He wanted his readers to understand how they had been hoodwinked by the false teachers' activities. There had been nothing magical or hidden when Paul had described to the Galatians in graphic detail the crucifixion and resurrection: *'It was before your eyes that Jesus Christ was publicly portrayed as crucified'* (3.1b)! In his preaching to the Galatians, Paul's dramatic presentation had been so vivid that it seemed to them that they had been eyewitnesses of the crucifixion (3.1b). Can they now be so foolish (3.2a) as to have turned away from everything that Christ's sacrifice meant for them?

PAUL'S RETORICAL QUESTIONS
These Celts had received the Holy Spirit (3.2-3). Surely that experience was very special. Paul used rhetorical questions to teach the people to think for themselves. He showed it was illogical for the Galatians to expect to live an even fuller Christian life by keeping the Law. Just as there were five Books of the Law, he asked the Galatians five questions that they should consider carefully.

QUESTION ONE
Firstly, Paul asked, *'Did you receive the Spirit by works of the law or by hearing with faith? ³Are you so foolish'* (3.2b,3)? He reminded the Galatians that after being saved through faith they had experienced the New Covenant activity of the Holy Spirit. We are not told if they had been

baptized by the Holy Spirit,[22] but his point was that the Old Covenant was superseded. The New Covenant had come with the crucifixion and resurrection. From the beginning of their new lives the Holy Spirit sanctified them as believers. How foolish to turn their backs on such a gift from God! Paul found this difficult to understand.

Working and Serving are Not the Same
We, too, should not think that after we are justified our work for God must begin, that we need to work to gain God's Brownie points as our reward. He is in control and it is through His grace that we are justified, and it is through His grace that we are sanctified now we live in the Spirit. Working and serving are two totally different concepts.

1. Working for the Lord: We want to work for God and think it is our duty to act and speak and think for Him. Then we expect to receive our reward. What presumption! We need to understand that God's justification and sanctification are given to us freely through His love and grace. That is why it is important that we do *not* work for God. If we follow the line of thinking that it is imperative that we work for God, we will not be following Christ.

2. Serving the Lord: Jesus said, '*If anyone serves me, he must follow me*' (Jn.12.26). Yes, we are told to '*Serve the Lord with gladness*' (Ps.100.2). As justified and sanctified Christians, our nature has changed and we serve Him but that is different from working for Him. We wait on Him for direction and we serve to show our love and gratitude. We do not serve in a way that suggests God could not do it Himself, if He chooses. We need to take care that we do not serve in a way that suggests we think we are indispensable. That attitude leads to pride in our own achievements.

---

[22] *See* Acts 19.6

Saved by Not Working
Our lives hang on not working for God. Think about it: workers do not receive gifts; they are paid a wage. If we want to receive God's lasting gifts of justification and sanctification, we dare not work, but if we yield and follow Him in love we can serve, if that is His plan for us.

There's a story about a young man who was proud of his prowess as a canoeist. He loved to go paddling. One day he decided to try a new river and enjoyed the scenery as he paddled downstream. Along the banks he saw fishermen with their rods and groups of people picnicking. Then he noticed people waving and beckoning, but he was happy and ignored them. Suddenly he realized he no longer had control of his canoe; the current was pulling him. Not far ahead he saw jagged rocks and heard the rush of an unseen waterfall below. He began to paddle quickly, but no matter how hard he tried, he could not reach the shore. Then someone threw a rope. It splashed into the water. A man shouted, "Drop your paddle! Grab the rope!" Reluctantly, he dropped his paddle. It disappeared in the swirling waters. The rope was thrown again and this time he caught it and was pulled to safety - just in time!

In the waters of life we cannot save ourselves no matter how hard we paddle, but when we stop struggling and grasp Christ's outstretched hand we are saved. It is not through our work, but in yielding that we receive salvation.

QUESTION TWO

Paul marvelled at the Galatians lack of good sense. He asked: *'Having begun with the Spirit, are you now being perfected with the flesh'* (3.3)? These Celts had begun their new spiritual life with the Holy Spirit who was working to perfect them. How can they imagine they could reach perfection by turning back and depending on the flesh? As in our story, the Galatians could only reach perfection and safety in God when they stopped relying on their own efforts and yielded to Him. It is the same for us today, whether we are Celts, or not. To be acceptable to God we must invite and welcome the Holy Spirit into our lives.

QUESTION THREE
Paul urgently demanded, *'Did you suffer so many things in vain? – if indeed it was in vain'* (3.4). Did you experience so much for nothing? He could not believe that all the Galatians experienced had been in vain. He wanted these Gentiles to direct their attention back and think about what had happened when they responded to his preaching. Then he asked, 'Does your conversion count for nothing, so now you want to turn away from my teaching?' If we ask ourselves this question, what will be our reply?

QUESTIONS FOUR AND FIVE
Finally, Paul asked his readers a double-barrelled question: *'Does he who supplies the Spirit to you and works miracles among you do so by the works of the law, or by hearing with faith'* (3.5)? The two parts of this question are two separate questions that need to be answered separately.

1. **THE FIRST PART, THE SPIRIT**:
   We can read the first part of the question as:
   'Does God supply you with the Spirit ... by your doing the works of the law, or by your believing what you heard?'
   As we have seen, neither the Galatians long ago nor we today can receive the Holy Spirit as a result of obeying the Law. We can only receive the Holy Spirit into our lives through our faith in Jesus Christ. For Paul, it was imperative that the Galatians believed the message that he brought them and knew in their hearts that it was the truth. To receive the Holy Spirit they needed to believe in the redeeming power of faith in Christ, as we, too, need to do today. Without the Holy Spirit in our lives, we are not Christians.

2. **THE SECOND PART, MIRACLES:**
   We can read the second part of the question in a similar way: *'Does God ... work miracles among you by your doing the works of the law, or by your believing what you heard?'*
   God does not work powerful miracles, either with the Galatians so long ago, or with us here, on the basis of our attempting to work in obedience to the Law. God's miracles can only take place through our implicit faith and trust in Him through our mediator, Jesus Christ. This was preached and taught by Paul and continued to be taught by Spirit-filled Christian leaders through the ages.

To put our faith in Jesus Christ is indeed the key.

To Think About or Discuss

1. How did the Galatians receive the Holy Spirit in their lives?

2. What was, and is, the criterion for salvation? How important was your conversion for you?

3. What was the choice that Paul offered the Galatians?

4. What is the New Covenant and why was it introduced?

5. Discuss Paul's reasons for differentiating between work and service.

≈11≈

ABRAHAM, FOREBEAR OF JEW AND GENTILE
CHAPTER 3. 6 - 9

3 *⁶Just as Abraham "believed God, and it was counted to him as righteousness," ⁷know then that it is those of faith who are the sons of Abraham. ⁸And the Scripture, foreseeing that God would justify the Gentiles by faith, preached the gospel beforehand to Abraham, saying, "In you shall all the nations be blessed." ⁹So then, those who are of faith are blessed along with Abraham, the man of faith.*

Paul cited Abraham as the spiritual forebear of both Jew and Gentile: all nations are to be blessed when they follow his example and put their faith in God.

FAITH AND GOD'S GRACE
In verses 6–9: Paul issued a second direct appeal to the Galatians. It was not just their own experience of receiving the gospel by faith that taught them that salvation could not be achieved by obedience to the Law, but it is through faith and the blessing of God's grace. God's grace cannot be earned; it is freely given.

The following story may help us to understand this more:
One Saturday, a man who had visited a local farmers' market was returning home on the bus. On his lap was a basket full of the delicious fruit he had bought.

At one stop a woman boarded the bus and sat down in the empty seat next to him. She admired the fruit and asked him where he had bought it.
When he told her, she said,

"I wish I'd thought of going there. I'm on my way to visit some friends and fruit like that would have made a perfect gift."
"Oh," said the man, "Would you like to have it?"
The woman thought, 'I'd love to, but I can't accept it. I don't even know the man.'
"That would be lovely," she replied, "If I can pay you for it."
"I'm sorry," said the man, "I'm happy to give it to you, but you can't pay me for it."
"I'd love to have it, but only if I pay," said the woman.
The man replied,
"You may only accept it as a gift, or not at all."
Eventually the woman accepted the gift and gave her thanks.

We are like that woman. So often we think we must work to pay God for our salvation and we are unwilling to accept it as His free gift. However, our salvation is given through His grace and if we don't accept it as a free gift, we cannot have it at all. And through our own foolish obstinacy we may perish.

Paul wrote to the Galatians that it was only through genuine faith and acceptance of God's gift of His Son that they could be counted as righteous. In his letter he used the history of Abraham as his example. Belief, faith in God, and acceptance of His gift was all that He needed to count Abraham as righteous.

When we lived in Papua New Guinea we found a good example of this. In the Dobu language there were two words for a gift. One was for when a gift was given and a bigger one was expected back in return. The other word, *oboboma*, was the word that stuck in our minds. It meant a gift given in love. Nothing was expected in return, in fact, to offer a gift in return was an insult to the giver. The *oboboma* had to be accepted with love and humility.

It would have been pointless for Paul to refer to Abraham so abruptly unless he was sure that the Galatians knew his story. Perhaps while Paul and the team were there they had taught them the early history of the Old Testament Scriptures. They may have even left the Galatians with copies of some of the Scrolls, or perhaps there were Jews living nearby, as there were in many towns and cities, and they had learnt about Abraham from them.

GOD'S PROMISES TO ABRAHAM

Long ago, God made what we call The Abrahamic Covenant with Abraham. In it God promised that the Messiah should spring from his seed, his descendants. This promise was given to Abraham because God had told him to leave his own country and his father's house and travel on a dangerous journey across other nations' territories to settle in a strange land, and, through his faith in God, Abraham obeyed, uprooting his whole family.

Paul wrote that Abraham *'believed God and it was counted to him as righteousness* (Galatians 3.6). This was a quote from Genesis 15.6: *'And he believed the Lord, and he counted it to him as righteousness.'* Abraham believed God's promises and God regarded it as righteousness. At that time there was no Torah, the Law that God later gave Moses. Paul is showing the Galatians that the Law was not necessary for being made right with God.

Paul used this precedent to show that God's promises to Abraham are for all who *'hear with faith,'* not just the people of Israel (Galatians 3.1-29). There had been no Law in the time of Abraham; it was not necessary for him, as he was righteous. However, the Law was introduced later and at that time it had an important purpose, but Paul saw that it was not necessary for the Gentiles. Those who believe are blessed, regardless of the Law and they are just as blessed as if they are descendants of Abraham (Galatians 3.7).

THE ABRAHAMIC COVENANT WAS BY FAITH

Abraham was accepted by God on the basis of faith and God promised him that '*in you all the families of the earth shall be blessed*' (Genesis 12.3). Or, as Paul wrote it, '*In you shall all the nations be blessed*' (Galatians 3. 8). Paul brought this closer to home later in his '*Letter of Paul to the Romans*' where he wrote to '*all those in Rome who are loved by God and called to be saints*' (Romans 1.7).

Furthermore, in Romans 4.1-25, Paul highlighted the point that, although Abraham was father of the Jews through his Covenant with God, as Christians who live in the age of the New Covenant we can claim to be part of Abraham's Covenant. The promise was that all nations of the earth would be blessed (Genesis 12. 3b), whether we are Jew or Gentile, through our faith as believers. Abraham's true descendants are those whose standing before God rests on faith in God's promise; this was how the promise to Abraham that all nations would be blessed through him finds its fulfillment and it continues to be relevant for us today through our faith in Jesus Christ and it is for everyone, including the Gentiles.

Remember the story of Abraham and his only son (Genesis 22.1- 18): to test his faith, God asked him to sacrifice his son, Isaac. Abraham, although heavy of heart, had such faith in God that he prepared to obey and at the last minute God provided a substitute, a ram caught in a nearby thicket.

If someone we knew and loved were to be put to death for an offence, would we offer to be a substitute? I doubt it. We are all sinners and deserve nothing but hell, not for just one offence, but for many we commit against God's laws.
I may think,
'Well, I've never murdered anyone, so my sins are not so very bad.' That's not true. My sins, even those that in my own eyes are small ones, cut me off from our holy God.

We cannot, of ourselves approach near to such a holy God and the only alternative to Heaven is Hell. But just as God provided a substitute for Abraham's son, Isaac, He loves us so much that He has provided a substitute for me and for you. Jesus, who was sinless, became the Lamb without blemish who was sacrificed for our sins.

Jesus Christ obeyed His Father God and offered Himself as a substitute for our sins, so that when we accept this, the greatest gift of all, we can claim Him as our Saviour and be forgiven and made righteous before God. Something so complex becomes simple when God opens our eyes to see that substitute.

The Law demands justice, but the Gospel offers mercy when we have faith.

GOD WILL FULFIL HIS PROMISE

Someday that promise of God to Abraham will be fulfilled. We read in *'The Revelation to John'* that in his vision John saw *'a great multitude that no one could number, from every nation, from all tribes and peoples and languages, standing before the throne and before the Lamb'* (Revelations 7. 9).

Those who have faith will be justified, and counted as righteous. God's plan is to redeem people from all nations and to bless all nations through Christ, but there is still much work to be done in sharing the Gospel. There are countries where missionaries are forbidden to enter, and where national Christians continue to be persecuted, imprisoned and killed for proclaiming Christ. It is growing worse throughout the world. Sometimes we are horrified when we hear or read about the persecution that occurs between other religions and sects, but 80% of those who are persecuted in the world are actually Christians.

God is sovereign even where every attempt is made to eliminate Christianity and eventually, through our faith, John's vision of God's plan will come to pass.

ONLY BY FAITH

In this part of his letter, Paul told the Galatians that God's favour could only be received by their faith in His promise. Good works that are a result of obedience to the Law could never - in ancient times and still today cannot - achieve our justification before God. To even try to strengthen our acceptance by Him through our works is to negate our experience of His grace. Here Paul was again referring to the Scriptures that he knew, understood and loved so much to show that God's favour can only be received by faith in His promise. No amount of good works can obtain His favour.

This theme of the juxtaposition of faith and the Law carries on right through to Chapter 3, verse 14.

To Think About or Discuss

1. The woman in the story doubted whether she should accept the gift of fruit. How do we deal with doubt, especially if the are doubts concerned with their faith?

2. We are told that Abraham was considered righteous; but was everything he did right in God's eyes?

    - How many other stories can you think of in the Scriptures where men or women were held up as examples, but did not always live in the right way?

3. Discuss the reasons why the Abrahamic Covenant continues when other promises in the Old Testament scriptures have been fulfilled or superseded?

4. Is there any way in which we can earn God's grace?

≈12≈

LIVE BY FAITH OR BE CURSED
CHAPTER 3. 10 - 14

3 *[10] For all who rely on works of the law are under a curse; for it is written, "Cursed be everyone who does not abide by all things written in the Book of the Law and does them." [11] Now it is evident that no one is justified before God by the law, for "The righteous shall live by faith." [12] But the law is not of faith, rather, "The one who does them shall live by them." [13] Christ redeemed us from the curse of the law by becoming a curse for us – for it is written, Cursed is everyone who is hanged on a tree" – [14] so that in Christ Jesus the blessing of Abraham might come to the Gentiles, so that we might receive the promised Spirit through faith.*

Paul reiterated that the Law cannot save, it can only condemn (3.10-12). He commenced with a strongly negative attitude towards relying on the Law for justification and this theme continues until verse 14. This negativity is concerned with the law of life and death. There are only two choices:
- The Torah[23] and the curse of death
- The death of Christ and eternal life

THOSE WHO RELY ON THE LAW ARE CURSED
When Paul wrote that those '*who rely on works of the law are under a curse*' *(*3.10), he meant that if we rely on the

---

[23] Torah: The name of the Law of God as recorded in the first five Books of the Old Testament, and these five are known as the Pentateuch

Law we are all cursed and condemned, because everyone breaks the Law; it is impossible to obey the whole of it.

Those who look for righteousness through the Law are imprisoned by sin (Galatians 3.22) and so put themselves under a guardian (3.25). In the Book of Leviticus we read, *'Whoever does the works of the law will live by them'* (Leviticus 18.5); to use the Law as a means of obtaining salvation is self-defeating. Again in Deuteronomy (27.26) we read: *'Cursed is everyone who does not observe and obey all the things written in the book of the law.'* Deuteronomy 28.1-14 sets out the blessings for obedience, not to the Law, but by being faithful to God (Deuteronomy 28.1-14), but it continues with the many curses that will fall on those who *'will not obey the voice of the Lord your God or be careful to do all his commandments'* (Deut. 28.15 on). Reliance on the Law can only lead to putting ourselves under the curse of death.

Paul's training in the Torah under Gamaliel in Jerusalem is so evident here. It shows the way he was taught to think in a logical manner. Recently, a friend in Taiwan asked me to teach her daughter, via emails, the Western way of debating. I explained that this requires the use of logic and deductive reasoning. In it's basic form we reduce thought to premises that are known as syllogisms. Although there can be more than three premises, a basic syllogism is composed of three parts: a major premise, a minor premise and a conclusion. If all the premises are true, then the conclusion must, of necessity, be true also.

We can see this kind of thinking so clearly here in Paul's argument that he based on Deuteronomy 27.26:
- Everyone who does not obey everything in the Law is cursed.
- No one can always obey the whole of the Law perfectly.
- Therefore everyone is cursed.

Through the use of logic and by providing four examples from the Old Testament Scriptures, Paul set out his argument to prove the fallacy of the visiting preachers' logic that was so confusing for the Galatians.

THE RIGHTEOUS SHALL LIVE BY FAITH

In Chapter 3.11 Paul concluded, *'Now it is evident that no one is justified before God by the law; for "The righteous shall live by faith."'* Here he was quoting Habakkuk 2.4: *'but the righteous shall live by his faith.'*

Paul needed to show the Galatians that it was impossible to achieve righteousness through the Law, but those who, through faith are made righteous, will live.

In verse 3.12, *'But the law is not of faith,'* Paul cited Leviticus 18.5 to stress his point. He discussed the same thing here as he did later in his *Letter to the Romans* (10.5) where he also quoted Leviticus 18.5. The one who does the Law shall live by the Law. Paul saw Leviticus 18.5 as a summary of the Law and juxtaposed it to justification and salvation. It highlights the difference between Jews and Gentiles; the Jews are under the Law, but it cannot save them, whereas the Gentiles are free and should claim that freedom.

There is something else behind Paul's thinking here: he has set simple faith in God through Jesus against the old need for obedience to the Law, the need to act in certain ways, the *'works of the law.'* But this becomes a curse because it is impossible to do and it cannot obtain justification for its followers. By turning to the Law, the Galatians were turning away from God's grace, His gift to them in Jesus Christ. It also infers that there was no real purpose in the crucifixion. If they followed the Law, then Jesus died for no purpose.

The Law offered life to those who kept it, but no one could keep it, so no on could gain life by attempting to follow it. Jesus' sacrifice on the Cross rendered the Law obsolete; He fulfilled the law and He is the way, the only way, to freedom and eternal life.

CHRIST BORE THE CURSE IN OUR PLACE

The divine Curse is the result of disobedience (3.10); it is impossible to obey the whole of the Law all of a person's life, so those who follow it incur God's curse. Christ is the one who redeems us from the curse of the Law and it is through Christ that Paul died to the Law. *'Christ redeemed us from the curse of the law by becoming a curse for us – for it is written, "Cursed is everyone who hangs on a tree'* (3.13).

Praise God that the curse of the Law was lifted by Christ's work on the cross when he received the curse in our place. Paul saw that it was truly fallacious thinking to imagine that by following the Law the Galatians would be saved. It simply could not occur. The only way to freedom and eternal life was to be free of the Law through the death of Christ.

In Christ's death on the cross there was both life and death. Christ went alive through the experience that bearing our sins meant, and it was only when He cried *'It is finished'* that *'he bowed his head and gave up his spirit'* (John 19.30). In that horrendous ordeal which culminated in death He entered a terrible suffering that man had never experienced before, as the holy Son of God was made a curse in our stead; His death so that we can avoid the curse and gain the blessing of life.

THE PROMISED SPIRIT SENT THROUGH FAITH

Through Isaiah's prophecy, God had promised '*I will pour my Spirit upon your offspring, and my blessing on your descendants*' (Isaiah 44.3b). The coming of the Spirit promised by God, the living presence of God came with the New Covenant, *'so that in Christ Jesus the blessing of Abraham might come to the Gentiles, so that we might receive the promised Spirit through faith* (Galatians 3.14). This was fulfilled at Pentecost when the Holy Spirit, the living Presence of God, came down on the believers gathered there.

GETTING IT STRAIGHT
Paul was urgent in his wish that the Galatians might understand this and get it straight in their hearts and lives.

Before he followed his brothers and migrated to Australia, my Cornish Grandfather did an apprenticeship. As he humorously put it, he 'served his time' at the Plymouth Dockyards as a cabinet-maker. He loved to read and when the 1881 census was taken he was living back at home in Par. A favourite book of his, published a few years before, in 1876, was *The Adventures of Tom Sawyer*, so, as his name was Thomas, with typical Cornish humour he told the census-takers that his occupation was Sawyer.

Let me tell you a little about Grandpa. He arrived by ship in Queenscliff, Victoria, on 26th February 1884, reached Melbourne the next day and had found work by the 29th. He worked at night to improve himself, studying mathematics in the evenings at the Working Man's Institute, a forerunner of the RMIT University, and then studied architecture at the North Melbourne School of Art, gaining second prize in 1888. In 1889, he married at the age of twenty-seven. He had drive, but he was also humble.

As a small child I learned to love the smell of the different woods in Grandpa's workshop and to handle some of his tools, including the straightedge. He had also learned so much of the Bible by heart and he would recite to me whole chapters. He was very concerned about my getting straight just what life was all about.

PAUL AND THE RIGHT ANGLE

By the time I was four, Grandpa had taught me to recite the Ten Commandments (Deuteronomy 5.7-21). They are the basis of much of the law of many countries, but Paul saw them from a different angle. He pointed out to the Galatians (3.10) that we cannot be saved by the Law, but only condemned by it. In Deuteronomy (27–28) we read many more laws and of the curses that come upon us if we do not keep them and yet it is impossible to do so. We need to see them from the right angle.

Jesus quoted Deuteronomy more than any other book of the Old Testament Scriptures. He warned that we break the Law, not only by our actions, but also by our thoughts.
- Do we worship God alone? What about our favourite film star or football player?
- We may not commit adultery in action, but what about in our thoughts?
- Do we see a neighbour with the latest ipad or technological gadget and wish so much that it was ours? That is coveting.

How, then, can we align our living to the right angle? As we have seen, Habakkuk (2.4) wrote that righteousness cannot be achieved through the law; it can only be achieved by living our faith.

JUSTIFICATION AND RIGHTEOUSNESS

Righteousness and justification are long, very 'churchy' sort of words, but they have real meaning and are important steps in the process of achieving our salvation. I read recently of a church claiming to be Bible-centred, but I wondered: should they really be aiming to be Bible-based and Christ-centred instead?

- **Justification**: When I learned typing – the old way, with a typewriter – we were taught how to justify our work so that the line of print made a straight edge on both sides of the page. If we are to be justified with our Almighty God, we need to be absolutely straight – on all sides. Doing this by ourselves is impossible. In Biblical terms, this requires us to be in a perfect relationship with God.

- **Righteousness**: In Psalm 143.2, David wrote of God that *'no one living is righteous before you.'* God is perfect, and certainly we are not. Can we achieve righteousness by being morally good, by doing good works, helping other people, attending church and supporting charities? NO! Salvation just doesn't work that way. Righteousness is being morally right and without sin.

Paul wrote (Galatians 2.16) that the only way we can be justified and made righteous, straight with God, is through faith in Jesus Christ. God justifies those who trust in Him through Jesus. It is only through God's grace, His unmerited favour, that we can accept His free gift of salvation through our faith in Jesus. It is a gift, not something that we can earn. When we accept this gift we can receive God's forgiveness, find release from our crookedness and guilt and be made righteous and justified. Then we can establish a true relationship with our God who is so straight, pure and holy. As Grandpa would have said, "That's what real life is all about."

To Think About or Discuss

1. Do you think that Paul's negative attitude to the Law is justified? Why?

2. Find some more of Paul's statements in his letter to the Galatians and apply deductive reasoning to them.
   Have you found any that are illogical?

3. Why do you think justification and righteousness are so important?

≈13≈

THE LAW AND THE PROMISE TO ABRAHAM
CHAPTER 3. 15 - 18

3 *¹⁵To give a human example, brothers: even with a man-made covenant, no one annuls it or adds to it once it has been ratified. ¹⁶Now the promises were made to Abraham and to his offspring. It does not say, "And to offsprings," referring to many, but referring to one. "And to your offspring," who is Christ. ¹⁷This is what I mean: the law, which came 430 years afterward, does not annul a covenant previously ratified by God, so as to make the promise void. ¹⁸For if the inheritance comes by the law, it no longer comes by promise; but God gave it to Abraham by a promise.*

In verses 15-18, Paul gave an example to show the Galatians that God's Covenant with Abraham was not annulled and, just as a person's will is a legal document and cannot be changed, God's promise is a legal covenant and cannot be changed either.

GOD'S COVENANTS WITH HUMANKIND

A covenant is a formal agreement between two parties. It may be a written agreement that is signed, like a will, or it may be a verbal promise, a commitment that once it has been made cannot legally be changed.

There were several covenants made between various people and God in the Old Testament Scriptures and together these ancient covenants make up what we call the Old Testament, or record of God's will. These covenants record the establishment of promises that were made between God and His people. There are references in the

Old Testament Scriptures to the fact that they were intended to be everlasting covenants, as, for example when we read in Isaiah 55. 3, '*I will make with you an everlasting covenant, my steadfast, sure love for David.*'

In the Bible, we can read about eight covenants and the first seven are all in the Old Testament, the first four in Genesis. We can view these covenants as pacts, special agreements that were made between God and Man.

1. **Edenic**: The word, 'covenant' is not used in Genesis 1.28. At this stage, humankind had not transgressed, so there was no need for law. This is the first pact between God and humans and in it He blesses and promises them dominion over every living thing on His created Earth.

2. **Adamic**: This promise does not mention a covenant either, but because Adam and Eve had broken the agreement that was made between God and His people, in Genesis 3.14-19, instead of a blessing God gives curses, which are for the serpent and for both Adam and Eve as representatives of all humanity.

3. **Noahic**: Genesis 8.20 to 9.17 describes the covenant that God made between Himself and Noah. It was established after the great flood when Noah built an altar to God. This covenant helped to restore the broken relationship between God and His creation, but recognized the barrier caused by the sinfulness of humankind. In it God blessed Noah and his descendants and all the creatures that came out of the ark. The rainbow was to become a sign of God's promise that never again would the whole earth be flooded.

4. **Abrahamic**: In this covenant we read in Genesis 12.1-3 that God told Abram to leave his homeland and go to another country. In return God would make of him 'a great nation' and that in him '*all the families of the earth shall be blessed.*' And, at the age of seventy-five, Abram obeyed God and trusted in Him.

5. **Mosaic**: When the Children of Israel were camped at Mt. Sinai, God gave Moses instructions and he obeyed them. This covenant is also known as the **Sinaitic Covenant**.

   The extensive Mosaic Covenant was recorded in what became known as the 'Book of the Covenant' (Exodus 24.7). It included the Ten Commandments (Exodus 20.1-17), instructions related to worship (Exodus 20.22-26), rules for the people's community life (Exodus 21.1 – 23.9), and directions about their entry into Canaan. Released from slavery, they had firm guidelines to follow. In return, '*all the people answered with one voice and said, "All the words that the Lord has spoken we will do"*' (Exodus 24.3b).

6. **Palestinian**: The Palestinian Covenant involved receiving God's blessings for obedience (Leviticus 26.1-13) and the punishments they would receive if they were disobedient (Leviticus 26.14-48). We have seen this repeated with the blessings for obedience in Deuteronomy 28.1-14, and God's curses for their disobedience in Deuteronomy 28.15-68. These punishments and blessings are carried further in Deuteronomy where we find that the concepts of repentance and forgiveness are introduced for the first time (30.1-10). God decreed that the people had a choice: to obey and live, or to disobey and die (Deuteronomy 30.11-20).

7. **Davidic**: God made a covenant with David, promising him that his throne would be established forever (2 Samuel 7.16), and in 1 Chronicles 17.7-8 God told David through the prophet Nathan that He had been with him since he was chosen as a shepherd boy and He would '*make a name for you, like the name of the great ones of the earth.*' He promised that He would give them a place to live in and that they would '*be disturbed no more*' (1 Chronicles 17.9).

8. **The New Covenant**: This is the meaning of '*The New Testament.*' In it we find the record of the New Covenant that God made with His people. The New Covenant was necessary because sinful humanity had caused the failure of the Old Testament Covenants: '*if that first covenant had been faultless, there would have been no occasion to look for a second*' (Hebrews 8.7).

In the *Letter to the Hebrews* the New Covenant is presented clearly in Chapter 8, where Jesus is described as the High Priest of the New Covenant. Verses 8-12 are a direct quote of a prophecy in Jeremiah 31.31-34, and verse 13 tells us that '*In speaking of a new covenant, he makes the first one obsolete.*' The old has passed away.

God made promises to Abraham on several occasions. It is thought that here in Galatians 3.16 Paul may have been referring to the promise God made to Abraham that he was giving all the land that he could see at that time to belong to him and his descendants forever (Genesis 13.15). However, it is more likely that he was referring to Genesis 16.19, when God promised to Abraham that he would establish a covenant with his, as yet only promised, son Isaac and his descendants, or offspring. Paul saw this as a prophecy, not that all Abraham's descendants would be myriad, but that one, special offspring many centuries later, would be Jesus Christ.

The fulfillment of these Old Testament covenants between Abraham and God was the promise of the Messiah.

THE ABRAHAMIC COVENANT IS NOT ANNULLED

In Galatians 3.17, Paul wrote that the Law came four hundred and thirty years after Abraham's Covenant with God. This time period could be ambiguous and may refer to the period when the children of Israel were enslaved in Exodus 12.40: *'The time that the people of Israel lived in Egypt was 430 years.'* This counts the period from Abraham to the exodus but that is not really about the Law.

More possibly, Paul was counting from God's confirmation of His promise to Jacob to go with him and make him into a great nation when he left Beersheba and went to Egypt. We can read about this Covenant in Genesis 46.3-4. This would then count the time in Egypt as the length of time from the 'Promise' to the 'Law.' This verse tells us that *'the law.... does not annul a covenant previously ratified by God, so as to nullify the promise.'*

Paul's point was that the Abrahamic Covenant was made before God gave people the Law and it was made through faith so the Law could not change it.

THE LAW IS FULFILLED

Paul pointed out in Galatians 2.18 that if we accept Jesus, through Him we are fulfilling the Law: *'If the inheritance comes by the law, it no longer comes by promise; but God gave it to Abraham by a promise.'* Therefore, if we try to restore the Law as a means of getting right with God then we become wrongdoers and breakers of the Law. Jews are offenders under the Law because they cannot help but break it, but as Christians we are fulfillers of the Law through our acceptance of Jesus' sacrifice for our sins.

The main point of this part of Paul's argument was that the promises God made to Abraham and to his offspring did not change when God gave Moses the Law. The Abrahamic Covenant remained and in spite of God giving Moses the Law, the prophecy would remain.

Many other laws came after the Ten Commandments and were necessary at the time, but were limited in what they could achieve. When Jesus Christ, Abraham's offspring, fulfilled that promise, He established the New Covenant for all people and nations. This included the blessing of the Holy Spirit and freedom from the Law. Through faith in Jesus' crucifixion and resurrection we can have forgiveness and freedom, and when we accept this wonderful gift our debt is paid; we are redeemed and can have fellowship with the Father. We need to remember that this freedom is not a licence to do as we please, but as our Father pleases.

To Think About or Discuss

1. Were any of the covenants made between God and humankind ever annulled? Why?

2. Discuss the making of a will.
    - Have you made a will?
    - Why should you do this?
    - Do you make it for yourself, or for others?
    - Can it be changed? If so, how?

3. Do you think that Paul's interpretation of Genesis 13.15 was correct, or does this carry the idea of its being prophecy too far?

≈14≈

THE PURPOSE OF THE LAW
CHAPTER 3. 19 - 24

3¹⁹Why then the law? It was added because of transgressions, until the offspring would come to whom the promise had been made, and it was put in place through angels by an intermediary. ²⁰Now an intermediary implies more than one, but God is one. ²¹Is the law then contrary to the promises of God? Certainly not! If a law had been given that could give life, then righteousness would indeed be by the law. ²²But the scripture imprisoned everything under sin, so that the promise by faith in Jesus Christ might be given to those who believe. ²³Now before faith came, we were held captive under the law, imprisoned until the coming faith would be revealed. ²⁴So then, the law was our guardian until Christ came, in order that we might be justified by faith.

In the early years of the recorded Bible, God revealed that His name is I AM, or YHWH. We usually add in the vowels to this name, but the Jewish girls to whom I taught Scripture some years ago wrote God's Name like that. They told me it was too holy a Name to be completely written and I found that very special. In those early times a lasting Covenant was made between Yahweh and Abraham.

WHY DID GOD GIVE HIS PEOPLE THE LAW?

While the Children of Israel wandered in the wilderness, Yahweh gave the people the Law because it was urgently needed at that time, but He never intended that it would last forever. '*Why then,*' asked Paul, 'did He give them the Law?'

THE PURPOSE OF THE LAW

Paul answered his own question. He explained that *'It was added because of transgressions'* (3.19). It was necessary for the spiritual wellbeing of God's people, but it was only given to them hundreds of years later because of their sinful ways.

The need for it highlighted their transgressions, their turning away from Him, their worship of false gods, or if they remembered God at all it was often just ritual and lip service, rather than true worship. Their infighting, unruly behaviour, cunning and deception showed how much the people needed to be saved from themselves; they needed a Saviour, one who could bring them back to what God intended them to be. This would be *'the offspring [who] would come to [those to] whom the promise had been made'* (3.19b).

God is so holy and pure, just and upright, and His children had become so crooked and corrupt and far removed from their special relationship with Him that they could no longer be called His children (Deut. 32.4-5). The Law was the only way to control them.

MEDIATORS AND MESSENGERS

Paul reminded the Galatians that through Moses, the Law was put in place by angels,[24] not just one or two, but *'ten thousands of holy ones'* (Deuteronomy 33.2). God chose

---

[24] Angels, messengers of God, are created spiritual beings (Psalm 104.4), but they can become visible in human form (Gen. 19.1 and several other places). There were many angels who were mentioned several times in both the Old and New Testaments. Gabriel is the first angel who was named in the Bible in Daniel 8.16, in 9.21 and in Luke 1.19 and 26. Michael, the archangel, is mentioned in Daniel 10.13, 21, in 12.1, Jude 9 and Rev. 12.7. Raphael is named in the Apocrypha in Tobit 5.4 and on.

Moses to be His intermediary, his mediator, for the children of Israel: *'These are the statutes and rules and laws that the Lord made between himself and the people of Israel through Moses on Mount Sinai'* (Leviticus 26.46).

A mediator is one who is placed in the middle to settle disputes. Here we see Paul's training in the Law; he clearly understood the legal inference of this originally Latin term for the means of conveying or influencing. But Moses was human and eventually died, although his influence lived on in the Scriptures for those who would listen and read.

THE PEOPLE'S REACTIONS

Through long years, God continued to send many mediators to convey both His love for His people and warnings against their sinfulness, but what was their usual reception? Remember that in Acts (7.53) Stephen, just before he was stoned, accused the people of killing the prophets God had sent to warn them of their waywardness. Most of these prophets had not been heeded and true fellowship with God was rare.

Paul's appointment by God as an apostle may have been to replace the martyred Stephen, as Paul's call is recorded in Acts 9. Paul pointed out that a mediator acts as a 'go-between' between two parties. Later James, the brother of John was killed (Acts 12.2).

Paul continued his letter, reminding the Celts that God then sent the promised Messiah, but this Messiah was part of God Himself. He took human form and came to earth as the promised Saviour of all humanity.

When we believe in God and put our trust in Him, who is One, His ultimate revelation does not come through an intermediary but from God alone: Jesus came as a man, but he is fully God. When we accept His sacrifice on the cross for our sins, we are forgiven, and when we put our faith in

Him, our relationship with God is restored and we become the sons and daughters of our Father God. What a privilege! Not just the Galatians, but we, too, as sinners and transgressors, can be made holy so that we can come close in fellowship with our loving Father.

Paul longs for these wayward Celts to understand the breath-taking reality of this and to grasp it with both hands and hold it tightly as the most precious thing that has ever been offered to them.

SALVATION IS THROUGH FAITH IN JESUS

Salvation in Christ is the result of God's promise, the New Covenant, not through the Law; it could never be through the Law. According to the promise made through the Covenant between God and Abraham, as Christ is God's Son those who put their trust in God, through his Son become His heirs.

Here, again, Paul was speaking as a lawyer. He told his readers that to rely on the Law was hopeless; the Law was not made with the intention to save, and it cannot save, that was not its purpose (3.19–24). Habakkuk 2.4 shows us that man can stand before God only on the basis of faith. Christ's acceptance of the curse of the broken law is the very basis through which the Gentiles might participate in the blessing of Abraham that Paul wrote about in Galatians 3.14.

The Law as given in the Scriptures does not ensure 'life' with God, as everything is imprisoned under sin's power: *'Is the law then contrary to the promises of God? Certainly not! If a law had been given that could give life, then righteousness would indeed be by the law'* (3.21).

Rather than enabling all Israelites to receive the promise, the Law was given so that the single 'offspring,' Christ, would receive the blessing. Therefore the blessing is obtained by our faith in Christ, not by being obedient to the Law. God was certainly not surprised that the Israelites were unable to obey the Law; in fact, at the end of the giving of the Law Moses foretold that the Israelites would not obey it (Deuteronomy 31.24-29). In this way the Law confirmed the promise to Abraham that justification could come only by faith (Galatians 3.6-9, 14, 18).

PUTTING FAITH IN CHRIST
If believing in His promises brings us closer to God, it should follow that putting our faith in Jesus Christ should be one of the easiest things we ever can do. Paul wrote, *'But the scripture imprisoned everything under sin, so that the promise by faith in Jesus Christ might be given to those who believe'* (3.22).

God has made this most vital decision that we can ever make in our lives easy for us to make and He places it within the range of possibility for everyone, from the strongest and richest to the weakest and poorest. Because believing is simply looking to Him and, through faith, claiming His promises for ourselves, it follows that putting our faith in Him can be done without any special aid except His Word. God planned that this one life-and-death decision would never occur as an accident; He fully intended it to be this way.

The decision to put our faith in Jesus can be done at any time and in any place; the time and place are unimportant; the decision is vital. To put our faith in Christ means that we can rest in Him and wherever we are, we are safe with Him. We only need to make that choice to love and obey Him in our hearts and our lives.

THE LAW AND DISCIPLINE
Before faith in Jesus became available to humankind, the Law was put in place to discipline His people: *'Now before*

faith came, we were held captive under the law, imprisoned until the coming faith would be revealed. So then, the law was our guardian until Christ came' (3.23-24a).

Paul continued his argument and explained that by 'faith' he meant New Covenant faith in Christ.[25] Paul used Abraham as an example of justification by faith (v 6-9, 12, 18), so he did not intend us to understand that there was no saving faith before Christ came. He meant that the Old Testament believers did not know about Jesus' finished work, and that was why the Law was so necessary.

A FREE CHOICE DECISION
Now the Galatians that Paul was so concerned about have been given the responsibility of free choice. He wanted them to understand that they must make the right choice and that was to choose to put their faith in Jesus Christ. It is the same for us. God gives us free choice too. Like those Celts almost two thousand years ago, when we put our trust in Jesus Christ, we become God's children and are no longer slaves; we are completely renewed. Let us now look at the Law that has been superseded.

FUNCTIONS OF THE LAW
The Old Testament Law was designed to be guardian of God's people and it had positive functions and was part of God's plan.

1. <u>To restrain and expose sin</u>. Its purpose was to make His people aware of sin and how to avoid it. This made the Jews *'under the law'* (3.23). By stating this, Paul meant that they were bound, or tied, to the demands of the Law. They were confined by it and their inability to keep it

---
[25]*See* verse 22

underlined the fact that they were, by nature, sinners.

It was as if the Jews were imprisoned by the Law, as they thought that justification could come through it, but we can see from both the Old and New Testaments that God did not intend the Law to be a means of salvation, it was to be their protector, their custodian.

2. To point to the promised Messiah. The Law also had another function and that was to point to the coming of the Messiah, the Christ. *'So then, the law was our guardian until Christ came, in order that we might be justified by faith'* (3.24).

When Christ came, through God's grace the discipline of the Law was no longer necessary.

In this passage Paul makes it quite clear that God never intended the Law to be a means of salvation. Its purpose was to prepare the people for the coming of the Messiah; it was to be their guide and custodian until Christ came. Then they could be justified by faith, thus fulfilling the function of the Law by convincing the people of the dangers of sin and their need of Christ.

To react wrongly to Paul's word of warning and to turn away from God's offer of grace can be truly fatal.

To Think About or Discuss

1. What is the most vital decision that we can ever make in our lives? If you have made this decision, why is it so important?

2. Discuss the reasons why God gave His people the Law?
   - Was it necessary?
   - Did it achieve the purpose that He intended? If not, why not?

3. Why didn't God intend the Law to be a means of salvation?

≈15≈

JUSTIFIED THROUGH FAITH
CHAPTER 3. 25 - 29

3. *[25] But now that faith has come, we are no longer under a guardian, [26] for in Christ Jesus you are all sons of God, through faith. [27] For as many of you as were baptized into Christ have put on Christ. [28] There is neither Jew nor Greek, there is neither slave nor free, there is no male and female, for you are all one in Christ Jesus. [29] And if you are Christ's, then you are Abraham's offspring, heirs according to promise.*

Paul and the missionary team had taught the Galatians about the importance of true faith in Christ so there was no need for others to come and teach them about the Law. In this part of his letter he stressed to them that to revert to the Law would be a retrograde step.

THE LAW HAS BEEN FULFILLED

The Law was a necessary and useful step forward as God's remedy for the Children of Israel as He taught them how to live within His plan for them. However, *'now that faith has come'* (3.25) through the crucifixion and resurrection of Jesus Christ, the Law was fulfilled and was no longer relevant. Children who were minors needed a guardian with them and God created the Law to be the guardian of His chosen people while they were immature and needed the restrictions provided by it. Those who put their faith in Jesus have no need of the Law as their guardian. They are God's adult children and have been freed from guardianship. This freedom is for all; they can become children of God when they put their faith in Jesus Christ. This is the way God established so humanity could achieve the maturity justification and righteousness.

That trust, that faith in Jesus, was so important. Paul told the Galatians that when they put their trust *'in Christ Jesus [rather than in the Law, they] are all children of God through faith.'* How wonderful that they could come close to God the Father and be adopted as His children! All that was needed was faith in the saving power of Jesus through His sacrifice on the cross and His resurrection.

It is the same for us today. When we put our faith and trust in Christ, God adopts us as His own children.[26] Life under the Law was like slavery where the child had to be obedient to the guardian, but now, through faith, life in Christ is marked by the freedom that comes from our being God's children.

BAPTISM: THE SYMBOL OF NEW LIFE

'For as many of you as were baptized into Christ have put on Christ' (3.27).

For Christians, baptism symbolizes death and resurrection. When believers are baptized, they go down under the water and die to the old life of the Law and death (Romans 6.3-4, Galatians 2.19; 6.14). Far back in the Old Testament Scriptures, people washed before prayer and sacrifice to show physical purity. Christian baptism is a symbol of spiritual purity and signifies the intention of the person being baptized to be a true follower of Jesus.

The person baptized comes up out of the waters, symbolically washed of his sins and made pure. By doing this, the baptized become participants in the new creation (2 Corinthians 5.17). Then they put on new, fresh, clothing, but it is so much more, as this symbolizes the putting on of Christ. It is the birth of a whole new life.

---

[26] The word used for 'children' here is a legal term that was used in the adoption and inheritance laws of first century Rome and Paul was quite conversant with these laws. Here and elsewhere in his letters (compare 4.5-7, Rom. 8.14-16, 23), this term refers to the status of all Christians, both male and female.

Baptism signifies that the person who is baptized is taking on a new life and purpose through being spiritually united with Christ. The baptized person is no longer a servant under the Law; he has taken on Christ into the whole of his being, not just externally, but spiritually as well. As Paul wrote earlier in his letter, all who grasp the faith can say with him, '*It is no longer I who live, but Christ who lives in me*' (Galatians 2.20). Hallelujah!

UNITY IN DIVERSITY

As a new creation, Paul declared that the one who was baptized was '*neither Jew nor Greek*' (3.28). The distinction between Jew and Gentile and any other difference had been removed, washed away (*see* Ephesians 2.11-22). Similarly, when we are baptized we become one with all others who have been baptized; we are united in Christ.

For us, as for the Galatians, baptism symbolizes that we are now adopted as God's children, and our old, sinful selves have passed away, we have died to our old lives and have been buried under the water. The old life has gone. Isn't that wonderful? It does not matter whether we are circumcised or uncircumcised, male or female, single or married, slave or free, the important thing is that we have chosen to put our faith in the saving power of our Lord Jesus Christ.

Here in his letter, Paul was emphasizing the point that these Gentile Galatian me, did not need to be circumcised and become Jews to be true Christians (*see* Galatians 3.14).

We need to remember that when Paul wrote that now there is '*neither slave nor free, there is no longer male and female*' (3.28), he was not implying that there were no differences in how these groups should interact and relate to each other, for in later letters he wrote about the differences that existed between slaves[27] and their master (Ephesians 6.5-89), and between husbands and wives (Ephesians 5.22-33). Rather, he was teaching that the old divisions and wrongful attitudes of superiority and inferiority had been abolished, *'for you are all one in Christ Jesus'* (3.28).

In writing this, he was teaching, not that when we come to faith and are baptized that we all become the same, that is obviously not so, and we are all endowed with different gifts, according to what God has planned for us. Paul does mean that within our God-created diversity there is unity; we have all become part of God's family, brothers and sister in Christ. That is something to be celebrated. Despite our differences, we are all one, united in the Church, the body of Christ Jesus.

CHILDREN OF THE COVENANT
Paul loved those Celtic Galatian converts and wanted them, as his brothers and sisters, to understand that the old, original Abrahamic Covenant still continues alongside the New Covenant; it has not passed away; it is not obsolete.

God's promise to Abraham and his seed was designed to last forever and it was for both Jew and Gentile. The coming of Jesus had ushered in the New Covenant, which is also to last forever, but the old Covenant still stands for everyone who grasps those promises. As Paul wrote:
'And if you are Christ's, then you are Abraham's offspring, heirs according to promise' (3.29).

Paul carried this thought further in his later letter to the Corinthians (1 Corinthians 7). It is not outward signs that are important, but what is in our hearts. When we are adopted into God's family, what joy! And, yes, we do receive those wonderful privileges and inheritance rights,

---

[27] Greek: bondservants

but we need to remember that we are also given the responsibility of being descendants of Abraham, and as children of the promise, we become heirs to that very same blessing of our Heavenly Father.

Paul concluded the points of this argument by reiterating that, in this unity he described, all Christians *'belong to Christ.'* He wrote this to the Galatians, but even as Christians today, we continue to be counted as Abraham's descendants and through faith in Jesus Christ we, as part of 'all nations of the earth,' can continue to receive God's great blessing.

God's promise so long ago still holds and as God's adopted children we also are inheritors and heirs of the promise. We are justified and made righteous before our holy Almighty Father through our faith in Him, *'according to the promise.'*

To Think About or Discuss

1 What do you know about adoption today? How different are our laws about adoption, or are they very much the same as they were in Paul's time?

2 In infant baptism the parents and godparents make the promises on the baby's behalf. As we are told that there is only one baptism, how can an older person remake those promises for himself/herself?

3 Discuss how unity in diversity can be achieved
    • within the family
    • within the church family

≈16≈

GOD'S FAMILY AND THE BACKSLIDING CELTS
CHAPTER 4. 1 - 12

In God's family, He is the Head, the Father. Those who are His children are His heirs, but they cannot receive their inheritance while they remain as minors under the Law.

4 *¹I mean that the heir, as long as he is a child is no different from a slave, ²though he is the owner of everything; but he is under guardians and managers until the date set by the father. ³In the same way when we were children, we were enslaved to the elementary principles of the world. ⁴But when the fullness of time had come, God sent forth his Son, born of woman, born under the law, ⁵to redeem those who were under the law, so that we might receive adoption as sons. ⁶And because you are sons, God has sent the Spirit of his Son into our hearts, crying, "Abba! Father!" ⁷So you are no longer a slave but a son, and if a son, then an heir through God ⁸Formerly, when you did not know God, you were enslaved to those that by nature are not gods. ⁹But now that you have come to know God, or rather to be known by God, how can you turn back again to the weak and worthless elemental principles of the world, whose slaves you want to be once more? ¹⁰You observe days and months and seasons and years! ¹¹I am afraid I may have labored over you in vain. ¹²Brothers, I entreat you, become as I am, for I also have become as you are.*

CHILDREN AND HEIRS
In this example, Paul was pointing out another way of looking at the situation the Galatians were creating for themselves. He wrote that under the old Covenant, the

Mosaic Law, it was true that they were heirs, but they were immature; they were just the same as minors and so *'no different from a slave'* (4.1).

In Roman law, if a son was heir to his father's property but was too young to receive his inheritance, he had no more status than a slave.[28] Guardians and trustees cared for all the heir's property and business dealings, and they remained under a pedagogue until they came of the age that had been set by the father. In those days, slaves were paid and if they could save enough they could redeem themselves and be freed, although quite often they remained in the same master's employment.

Paul claimed that it was the same for them: *'So with us;'* he and the Christians with him had been slaves. As a Jew he had been a slave under the Mosaic Law. For the Galatians, the elementary principles that had ruled them had been the basic concepts of their pagan religion. Because of these, they had been slaves in both their attitude of mind, their way of thinking, and in the way they lived. Now they had learned to put their trust in Jesus they were being enticed to go back and put their trust in the Law and return to slavery.

REDEEMED FROM UNDER THE LAW
Paul emphasized what a retrograde step that would be. He continued teaching: *'When the fullness of time had come'* (4.4) God sent his Son at exactly the right moment of time in human history. God's Son was born of a Jewish woman

---

[28] The word *slave* has changed greatly. A tribe once dwelt on the banks of the Dnieper, the fourth longest river in Europe. It begins in Russia, forms the border between Belarus and Ukraine and flows into the Black Sea. This tribe was called the Slavi as *slav* meant they were a noble, illustrious people. However, later in the Roman Empire many of them were captured and made servants all over Europe, so the word came to mean a slave.

and so He was born a Jew and under the Law. This was so He could reach God's chosen people, the Jews, with His message of redemption. Through His sacrifice, their debt was paid to the master and they were free to be adopted as children of God's family.

In Roman law, as it is with us today, a legal adoption meant that the person adopted became an heir and had the same status as any other children in the family. In Roman times it was the custom that if someone had no heirs they would adopt a grown person who was already mature, even a trusted slave, to become the heir.

Paul was also born a Jew, but following Christ's revelation to him on the road, he became a follower of Christ and so did not now see himself as a full member of Judaism; in later letters he sometimes referred to himself, not as a Jew, but as an Israelite (see 2 Corinthians 11.22). Through Christ's death he had died to the old Law and his old life; he now shared Christ's resurrection and was living a new life. He was no longer a slave under the Law, but was now an heir as he had been adopted into God's family.

BELIEVERS ARE GOD'S CHILDREN
Faith in Christ frees God's children forever from the need to seek salvation through doing the works of the Law. By God's grace, having trusted Christ as our Saviour, we who are believers have been brought into the very family of God. He has covenanted with us to be our God, and we are to be His people. Through Christ He has adopted us as His sons and daughters, His very own children, His family.

As a result of our being God's children, He has sent His Holy Spirit to live within us and to testify that we are His children: *And because you are sons, God has sent the Spirit of his Son into our hearts, crying, "Abba! Father!" So you are no longer a slave but a son, and if a son, then an heir through God.* (4.6-7). The Holy Spirit bears witness within us to this special relationship that we have with God when we come into His fatherly love and cry in our hearts, *'Abba! Father!'* What could be more wonderful!

In the Jewish household, the slaves were not allowed to use the word 'Abba,'[29] to address the head of the family. It was a word that was reserved for the family's children. Paul wrote further about this in his *Letter to the Romans* (8.14-17). His use of this word is intended to convey to us how deeply the Spirit assures us that when we become Christians we are indeed children of the Most High God, our Heavenly Father, so that we receive the inheritance, the promised Spirit of His Son.

God loves His children with a very special kind of love; it is a fatherly love. He calls us to be His chosen ones, holy and beloved. He promises to take great delight in us. He loves us because we have become His very own.

THE BACKSLIDING CELTS

Paul reminded the Galatians of what they had been like. Before coming to know the one true God, they had worshipped idols, creatures and objects in the natural world around them.[30] He could not believe they would now revert to enslavement to the dark world of fear and superstition.

HEATHEN GODS

Paul strongly reprimanded the Galatians. Before his mission, the Celts had lived in a world that was dominated by demonic spirits that controlled their former religions. He pointed out that those gods they had worshipped were

---

[29] 'Abba' is the Aramaic word for Father

[30] As well as their own gods, the Gauls worshipped Greek and Roman gods including Esus and Teurtates (the Roman Mars and Mercury) Taranes (Jupiter), Apollo and Minerva.

not real; they '*were enslaved to beings that by nature are not gods*' (4.8). If they turned back to that false way of life they would forfeit and abandon their newly found life as children of the one true God.

In fact, in 1 Corinthians 10.20 Paul went even further and referred to pagan sacrifice as being sacrifice to demons; people cannot eat food sacrificed to demons and then turn around and share together in the Lord's Supper. To lapse in this way is to go back and be enslaved all over again to an elementary, unchristian way of worship.

PAGAN SUPERSTITIONS OR TRUE WORSHIP

Do we, whether or not we are Celts, still allow ourselves to be enticed along wrong pathways and be drawn back into slavery today? We can so easily backslide into the lifestyle we had before giving our lives to Jesus.

We may be illogically afraid of something, or we may be superstitious – about a certain number, walking under a ladder, or any foolish notions. Do you ever turn to the 'Your Stars' page of a favourite magazine to find out what the following week is likely to bring? Do you find yourself being more interested in attending a football match than in attending worship at church?

These are pagan attitudes. Nothing is more important than our relationship with God and our corporate worship of Him, our worship together with others, the Body of Christ. We often seem to hear it said,
"Oh, yes. I believe in God. I just don't go to church. You can worship Him in the garden, in the bush, down by the sea, anywhere!"

That is true, we can worship Him in our hearts anywhere, but do we? Or is it just an excuse? We can have fellowship with our Father anywhere, but corporate praise and worship is important.

FELLOWSHIP WITH THE FATHER

These Celts had been shown the way to a wonderful, personal relationship with God, to be His children, knowing Him and being known by Him: They had *'come to know God, or rather to be known by God'* (4.9). Surely, once they had known the joy of a relationship with Father God, they could not possibly turn back to the spiritual poverty of the life that they had before.

When we know God as our Father, we, as His children, should be talking to Him about our problems, discussing them with Him and relying on Him and His grace to help us to find answers and to face whatever difficult situation may eventuate.

PAGAN FESTIVANS AND JEWISH CELEBRATIONS

In verse 10, Paul may have been referring to the days, months, seasons, and years of the Galatians' pagan festivals, or it could be that the false teachers had been insisting on their observation of days, months, seasons and years that were part of the ceremonial Laws of the Mosaic Covenant (*see* Leviticus 23.5, 16, 28; 25.4). Whichever it was, Paul stressed that these details were not the point.

The important thing was that they put their faith in Jesus, not that they allowed their lives to be ruled by a series of ritualistic observances. Nor should we. However, if we follow a liturgy the services can be carried out in an orderly fashion that honours God and we are free to worship with all our hearts.

WAS PAUL'S WORK FUTILE?

Paul pointed out that if the false teachers were trying to persuade the Galatians to live like Jews when they were

Gentiles and now Christians, it was absurd. If these new Celtic Christians turn and follow the Old Testament Laws they will forfeit the gospel of justification by faith alone. Paul felt that if this were the case then all his work had been futile:
I am afraid I may have labored over you in vain' (4.11).
Had he really wasted his time on this mission? There is no other way to be right with God, but through Jesus Christ alone.

PAUL AS A MODEL
Paul begged the Galatians to imitate what they had seen as they watched, listened and learned from him: *'Brothers, I entreat you, become as I am'* (4.12). He told them that he saw them as his brothers and sisters in Christ, blood relatives through Christ's precious blood and so much closer than a friend. He entreated them to be free from the bondage of Jewish ritualism and ordinances.

PAUL BECAME ONE OF THEM
Paul, who was born a Jew, had changed and become like these Galatians: *'I also have become as you are'* (4.12). Even more than Paul, they had no obligation to observe the many rules and regulations of the Jews. That is the way he was when he was with them and ministered to them. In this statement he implied the idea that he was praying that they would continue to embrace the message of salvation that he had brought them.

This is a great reminder that Paul is an excellent example for anyone involved in ministry or missionary work, or even being a 'good neighbour,' or sharing a faith story. If we are to build good relationships with those we work with or live near, we do need to become as one of them. The rapport between a minister, pastor, Christian church worker or member and the people that God has given them to guide, minister to, and lead, is so important.

I remember how delighted I was when we first arrived at our island destination where we were to work as missionaries in Papua New Guinea. It was stiflingly hot and everything looked so different from home, but as we stepped off the boat onto the wharf to shake hundreds of sweaty, welcoming hands, one lady patted my black hair and called out to the others:
"She's one of us!"

Immediately I felt that I was among friends. As yet I did not know any of them, but with those few words I was made to feel part of the community that I quickly learned to love and take to my heart.

As parishioners in our churches we need to be aware of welcoming newcomers, too, whether they come as enquirers, members, or priests and ministers. It can be a very lonely feeling to be in a new place and it can be our joy to welcome people and make them feel wanted and 'one of us,' brothers and sisters together as children of the Lord.

To Think About or Discuss

1 Why did Paul sometimes refer to himself as an Israelite, rather than as a Jew?

2 The African saint, St. Cyprian, wrote that the person who does not have the church as his mother does not have God as his father. Discuss this statement.

3 In the busyness of our daily lives, how can we find time for fellowship with our Heavenly Father? Is a daily Quiet Time spent with Him necessary for our spiritual health, or is attending worship once a week sufficient?

≈17≈

THE SIGNIFICANCE OF PAUL'S AILMENT
CHAPTER 4: 13 - 15

Paul reminded the Galatians of what had occurred when they first heard the gospel. They had willingly received the team and the message they brought. He also contrasted his own ministry with that of the false teachers and expressed his gratitude that when he was with them and suffered from a physical infirmity, they cared for him as if he was an angel or even Jesus Christ Himself. High praise!

4 ^{13}You know it was because of a physical infirmity that I preached the gospel to you at first, ^{14} and though my condition was a trial to you, you did not scorn or despise me, but received me as an angel of God, as Christ Jesus. ^{15}What then has become of your blessedness? For I testify to you that if possible, you would have gouged out your eyes and given them to me.

It appears that Barnabas, Paul and their friends had made their plans for their journey and were just passing through, intent on taking their mission elsewhere, but because of a bodily ailment that Paul had the misfortune to contract (4.13) as they were travelling though Galatia, he needed to remain there for a time to overcome it and recuperate.

GOD USED PAUL'S AILMENT
Because of his illness, God kept him there among these people. Paul wrote, '*it was because of a physical infirmity that I preached the gospel to you at first.*' While he needed to stay there, he took the opportunity to tell them about Jesus. It may not have been the original plan for the travels of the little missionary group, but it was part of God's plan for the redemption of these Celts.

God used Paul's ailment so that the Galatians could hear and receive the wonderful message of the Good News. How different the collection of Paul's Letters in the New Testament may have been otherwise.

PAUL'S AILMENT
The exact nature of Paul's ailment is unknown and there have been quite a few suggestions over time, and, for me, a couple sound plausible.

1. **Malaria**:
It is known that there was Malaria in the area. It is quite possible that the *anopheles* mosquito could have bitten and infected him with the parasite while they were travelling through the swampy coastland area and that by the time they had arrived in Galatia he had come down with this serious illness.

    During our years in the Papua New Guinea Islands, even with our regularly taking the prescribed prophylactics, all our family contracted Malaria at different times and, even with medicines and treatment that fever can be really nasty with high temperatures, sweating, vomiting and headaches. Without treatment, people around us died; they still do. How much worse that would have been for Paul in those days without access to our modern medications.

    Scientists still seek methods of eradication and treatment, but it continues to be prevalent in many countries even today. I have heard it said that in Africa little children die at the rate of one a minute from Malaria. Just from one small, annoying mosquito. How devastating and heart-rending for their parents and families!

It was around this time that John Mark decided to leave the group and return home (Acts 13.13). Perhaps the sight of Paul's illness was too much for him to cope with.

Probably because of Paul's disease and discomfort, the rest of the group turned aside from their planned route. This decision would have taken them inland to the hilly country of Galatia and away from the mosquito infected areas. Malaria is a possibility for what afflicted Paul.

2. **Conjunctivitis**:
Some researchers think that verse 15 clearly tells us that Paul's illness was connected with his eyes: *'For I testify to you that if possible, you would have gouged out your eyes and given them to me.'*

A problem with Paul's eyes could easily have caused great difficulty on their walking tour as the paths they took were hazardous and they each needed clear vision to avoid accidents. Paul's problem may have been conjunctivitis, which so often occurred and kept recurring. In those days it was very difficult to clear and remained so right up until later in the twentieth century.

When I was researching my family tree I discovered that my Grandmother, along with about half the school that she attended in Campbell's Creek, Victoria, at some time or other contracted conjunctivitis. I still have one of our family's eyebaths; it is made of glass, has a stem and is shaped rather like an oval eggcup. At that time conjunctivitis was a very contagious disease and the Education Department decreed that children so afflicted had to be excluded from school until it was cleared and, according to what

I read in the school records, that could take up to three weeks.

Conjunctivitis is a disease that is distressing for the patient and distasteful for others to see, as the eyes needed to be bathed frequently with saline solution to remove the sticky discharge that impaired the vision. Often the eyes had crusted up so much overnight that they could not be opened in the morning until the pus had been softened with warm, salty water; use of the eyebath was not sufficient.

Conjunctivitis is a disease that could have been easily contracted on their dusty walk and I think that pinpointing this, or something similar, as Paul's physical problem is borne out in verse 14. In it he wrote that although the condition was such a trial to his hosts they did not regard him as loathsome. These lusty Celts were not disgusted by his condition, but instead they ministered to his needs as their Celtic code of ethics demanded and they offered the missionary team hospitality. The Galatians took great care of Paul until he recovered.

SCOFFERS AND SCORNERS
In his praise of their kind treatment of him, Paul wrote:
"... and though my condition was a trial to you, you did not scorn or despise me, but received me as an angel of God, as Christ Jesus' (4.14b).

These volatile Galatians could easily have scoffed at his physical condition and scorned his message, too, but they did not, they offered him and the team their famous hospitality and cared for him in the best way they could.

Scoffers[31] and scorners seem to appear quite often in both the Old Testament and in the New Testament. We remember these, especially the prophesies in the Old Testament and then the actual happenings in the New Testament of the treatment of Jesus during his life-time and during His trial, just before the crucifixion.

Scoffing and scorning are concerned with a mental attitude and Paul was grateful that the people did not scorn him. Unkind words can hurt deeply and we can be made upset and unhappy by a chance derogatory or scornful remark. We can also hurt others in the same way with a careless word.

It has often been stressed that our mental capacity is not as important as our attitude. As members of God's church, we need to remember that a right attitude is what God requires from us.

There is a story I heard long ago about a meeting between a Fijian chief and an English visitor.

As they spoke together, the visitor expressed surprise that the chief accepted the missionaries' teaching.
He said scornfully,
"I would have thought that an intelligent person like you would not fall for all that Bible nonsense."
"Oh?" the chief retorted, pointing.

---

[31] Scoff is only mentioned once in the Old Testament, in Habakkuk 1.10, and scoffers and scoffing once each in the New Testament, both in 2 Peter.3.3. Scorn is mentioned 13 times in the Old Testament, e.g. Psalm 22.7, '*All they that see me laugh me to scorn.*' Scorner/s are mentioned 18 times in Proverbs, 5 in Hosea, 4 in Ezekiel, 3 in Isaiah, twice in Psalms and once in Job, and three times in the New Testament, all in the Synoptic Gospels and all connected with Jesus, although now it is often translated as 'laughed at him,' which does not carry quite the same meaning.

"See that big stone over there? That's what we once used to crush our enemies' heads.

"And see that oven there? That's where we cooked them for our feasts.

"If it weren't for the missionaries and the Bible, you'd be there right now. You should be thanking God for those missionaries and the Bible!"

To Think About or Discuss

1. Have you ever planned for something in your life and then found that God had shut the door on it?
   - How did that come about?
   - Did you later find that God's plan was better, but one that you would never have thought possible?

2. Does God cause certain adverse events to occur in our lives, or does he use those events to achieve a good outcome that is part of His plan?

3. How can we deal with people who scoff and scorn at our faith and belief in God?

≈18≈

SPIRITUAL GROWTH
CHAPTER 4. 16 - 20

All the good will that Paul experienced when the team was with the Galatians seemed to have evaporated.

4 *[16]Have I then become your enemy by telling you the truth? [17] They make much of you, but for no good purpose. They want to shut you out, that you may make much of them. [18] It is always good to be made much of for a good purpose, and not only when I am present with you, [19]my little children, for whom I am again in the anguish of childbirth until Christ is formed in you! [20]I wish I could be present with you now and change my tone, for I am perplexed about you.*

The Galatian Celts had offered Paul and the rest of the group their famous hospitality and had been kind to him – and had their ears and hearts open to listen to his message.

I don't know if Paul knew their history, but we do,[32] and we know that this wasn't the first time that the Celts had been turncoats. They had looked upon Paul as an angel from heaven, but now they were treating him as someone who had infiltrated the group and then deceived them.

THE TRUTH IS IMPORTANT
Paul now asked if he had become their enemy by dealing truthfully with them (4.16). I wonder if sometimes we can make enemies by being truthful. People do not always want to know the truth. That set me thinking: How important is it to tell the truth? Is it always necessary to deal truthfully

---

[32] See the Appendices

with others? What if it is detrimental to a patient's health if the doctor tells her the truth?

To bring closer the problem of whether it is necessary to tell the truth always, decide after you have read this story: Your wife has just bought a new jacket. She puts it on, does a pirouette and asks your opinion. Would you reply: "Well, Darling, it does poke out a bit and makes you look rather big at the back."
Definitely unwise!

There could be a word of warning here. We need to be sure we are not tempted to see ourselves in the best light, instead of being honest. Our minister expounds on wonderful Biblical truths, we agree with and think he is a great preacher, but when he turns to Scripture that is not so palatable, do we truly see ourselves as someone who has not done so well, or do we squirm in the pews and object in our hearts when a failing is pointed out?

SINCERITY

In some translations Paul asks if he has become their enemy by telling the truth and dealing sincerely with them. I love that word 'sincere.' I remember an elderly minister explaining it in the Children's Talk in church.

He told us about the sculptors in ancient Rome who created lovely figurines in beautiful white marble:
"Sometimes, after spending months on a statue, when nearly at the end of the work, the sculptor's chisel would slip, or some other disaster occur. If the sculptor were dishonest, he might fill the crack with wax and no one would notice the flaw until after the statue had been paid for and delivered miles away. Then the wax would melt in the hot sunshine and the blemish would be discovered. To ensure that the patron would know that the work was genuine and there were no hidden blemishes, the sculptor

would claim that it was '*sine cera*,' two Latin words that mean 'without wax, sincere.'"

How lovely that we often use that word at the end of a letter, "Yours sincerely," meaning, "In my letter I have been quite truthful; I am not covering anything up."

I loved that story. How important it is to be sincere in all that we say, write and do. Just to be sure I had remembered the story correctly I checked it on the Internet. One article claimed that this was an old wives tale, but when I looked up the Latin words, I found that the old minister had indeed known his Latin and that his story was – sincere - and true.

AVOID FLATTERY

Paul warned the Galatians that the Judaizing teachers were trying to dazzle them with all the attention they were bestowing on them, but he added:
"Take my word for it: they are making much of you '*for no good purpose*' (4.17). All this flattery is for their own ends. Their aim is to boost you so that you will flatter them in return and make them feel good. They have an underlying purpose that is not honourable, a hidden agenda. They just want to persuade you that I am wrong so they will avoid being persecuted by the non-Christian Jews and so gain favour in their eyes by your being circumcised."

The false teachers he had heard about were trying to isolate the Galatians with their flattery, and Paul exhorted them avoid it. The false teachers wanted to form an exclusive 'club' of people who observed Jewish ceremonial law and then shut the other Gentile Christians out. They were trying to persuade the Celts to take sides against Paul, to make them into an exclusive club of Christians who continued to observe the Jewish ceremonial laws and kept a foot in both camps. However, as Paul pointed out, these Celts were not Jews in the first place, they were Gentiles and there was no need for them to observe these laws.

CHRISTIANS AND CLIQUES

How often cliques can form in groups in the community, including within churches, and what problems these can cause! They may begin innocently enough with a group of people who, perhaps, are neighbours, work together, or share the same hobbies and interests. They may have attended that church since babyhood; they attended Sunday School, were confirmed there, sang in the choir and were married there. It is 'their' church. No! It is God's church and we are all God's children. The church is a family, and a family shares together; the members care about each one and they should help and encourage each other.

UNHAPPY MEMBERS

Are there people in your church who are restless, even upset and angry? Are they thinking about changing churches because the new minister doesn't do things the way the old one did? Again, this can lead to cliques of critical folk who gossip and complain to each other. Sure, while a new minister coming into a church may feel that he needs to be the proverbial new broom that sweeps clean, it is not always the wisest action. The congregation may have a certain level of churchmanship, traditions that they are most comfortable with and he needs to respect these.

There can be other, more gentle ways of bringing in change if it is really going to be best for this particular group of people. It is important to be sensitive to the needs of the people; the minister may move on again in a few years and what will happen then? The minister is the leader, but it is the people who are the Church, the Body of Christ.

SOLVING THE PROBLEM

If you are disgruntled and unhappy, and even thinking of changing your allegiance to another church: instead of getting into a group, a clique of clerical criticizers, what about forming a group that prays for the minister instead? He has many problems to deal with, people to help, priorities to sort out and a great desire to lead, as God would have him do. How much better to offer him the hand of friendship and support him in prayer!

MAKE MUCH OF YOUR HORSES

In verse 18 Paul wrote: *'It is always good to be made much of for a good purpose.'* He understood how the new teaching was tempting the Galatians. It was appealing that these teachers were enthusiastic in wanting them on their side, but he reminded them that they needed to look at the group's purpose. What were their motives?

Later, when he wrote to the Thessalonians (5.11), Paul continued this idea: *'Encourage one another and build one another up.'*

To make much of people can be a good thing. This reminds me of a story my father told:

In World War I, as he was a scale-maker in the family business, he had learned meticulous precision work so he joined the engineers.
Once they reached France, he found that his job was to keep a canon in good order and to care for the horses that pulled it. When they returned from the battle, the last order before rubbing down the horses and feeding them was
"Make much of your horses!" That was an important order and although horses do not play a part in most of our lives today, this story is a good reminder for us to make much of the people we live and work with. All of us are ministers to others around us and at the same time we are ministered to in various of ways. We need to remember to thank and make much of those who help us serve the Lord together.

SPIRITUAL GROWTH

Paul was deeply concerned for the Galatians; he regarded them as precious children, but children need to grow and these Celts had not been growing spiritually (4.19-20). When he was with them, he had the joy of seeing them being born again when they made their decision to put their faith in Jesus and this, their wonderful rebirth, was for him like the pain of childbirth, he felt so deeply for them.

When he left Galatia the members of the fledgling churches had been growing well spiritually, but it was obvious that now they had regressed and become like little babies again. Because of these problems that had come up, their growth was becoming more and more stunted. Paul felt this personally and profoundly; he wrote that he was again suffering the pangs of birth for them. His prayer was that Christ would be permanently formed within them, that they would grow to be moulded and shaped like Christ.

Paul wrote: *'until Christ is formed in you'* (4.19). He prayed that the Galatian believers would emulate Christ's redemptive self-giving until He was truly formed in them and they had learned to live to become like Him.

SPIRITUALITY AND RELIGION
We sometimes hear of people who are interested in 'spirituality,' but they are 'not religious' and do not want to have anything to do with religion. However, the spirit is the opposite of the physical and material, and human spirituality is inescapably bound up, interlocked, with religion. It may not be the Christian religion, but there is no closing our eyes and ears – or our minds - to the fact that it is the way that God has created us. Spirituality and religion are inherently fused together in our psyche.

Once, I heard it explained this way: the spirit is like water, but water uncontained is useless. Put it in a glass, or even in our hands, and it can quench our thirst. When the Holy Spirit comes into our lives when we have given them to Jesus, our spiritual spring is contained and directed, and then we can begin to drink and grow spiritually.

Spiritual growth is important for Christians of every age and condition. It may be wonderfully exhilarating to claim to be born again and beautifully comfortable to rest as a babe in Christ, but it is not good enough to remain there. We need to learn to grow and become mature Christians.

Actually, I could change the analogy and say that spiritual growth can be likened to a lovely flower coming into bloom. A tiny bud appears and slowly grows. But as it grows it may be scarred by blight or mutilated by snails so that it remains a tiny bud until it dies and falls off the stem, or it may continue to grow and slowly mature until that moment when, at last, it opens fully to be embraced by the sunshine.

If we keep the blight and snails at bay, avoid the things that pull us away from the Light, and keep on growing and maturing, then, when we reach God's wonderful everlasting light with Him, that is when we open up fully to His Light and become fully mature in life everlasting.

AN ONGOING PROCESS
The new spiritual life is an ongoing process in which we continue to develop and grow all our lives.

How can we grow spiritually?
- By reading God's word to increase our knowledge and understanding of the importance of our relationship with Him.
- By becoming more aware of sin in our lives and working to eradicate that sin and bad habits as much as possible.
- By modelling our lives on Jesus and following His example. He was truly spiritual.
- By increasing our faith and trust in our Father God.

There are more ways, too, but to begin with we need to be aware that as Christians, through our faith in Christ we are new creations. Remember that Paul later carried further the idea of being babes when he wrote to the Corinthians (2 Corinthians 5.17) that if we are in Christ we are a new creation; what is past in our old lives is gone; we put it behind us.

We must look forward in faith, but, like the bud, a new creation does not stay still, if it is fed and watered, it grows and develops; this is a whole lifetime commitment. If we stagnate and stand still, we're likely to drop off the twig – our spiritual life dies. We must continue to grow spiritually all our lives and always be open to learn more, to heed God's rebukes when we stray, and to equip ourselves so we can open up and blossom, showing our thanks by being involved in every good service of which we are capable.

To Think About or Discuss

1. How necessary is it to tell the truth in every situation? Are there ever any occasions when it would be acceptable to avoid doing this?

2. Think about the story behind the word 'sincere.' Why is it important to be sincere?

3. To what extent do you think it is true that spirituality and religion are bound together? Why is this?

4. Can we become spiritually mature in this life, or is it only when we die physically that we can reach real maturity?

≈19≈

HAGAR AND SARAH AS ALLEGORY
CHAPTER 4. 21 - 31

4 [21]*Tell me, you who desire to be under the law, do you not listen to the law?* [22]*For it is written that Abraham had two sons, one by a slave woman and one by a free woman.* [23]*But the son of the slave was born according to the flesh, while the son of the free woman was born through promise. Now this may be interpreted allegorically: these women are two covenants. One is from Mount Sinai, bearing children for slavery; she is Hagar.* [25]*Now Hagar is Mount Sinai in Arabia; she corresponds to the present Jerusalem, for she is in slavery with her children.* [26]*But the Jerusalem above is free, for she is our mother. For it is written,*
> *"Rejoice, O barren one, who does not bear;*
> *break forth and cry aloud, you who are not in labour!*
> *For the children of the desolate one will be more than those of the one who has a husband."*

[28]*Now you, brothers, like Isaac, are children of the promise.* [29]*But just as at that time he who was born according to the flesh persecuted him who was born according to the Spirit, so also it is now.* [30]*But what does the scripture say? "Cast out the slave woman and her son, for the son of the slave woman shall not inherit with the son of the free woman."* [31]*So brothers, we are not children of the slave but of the free woman.*

Paul returned to again emphasize the difference between being a free child of God through the sacrifice of Jesus, and being a slave to the Old Testament Covenant Law, which among other things, highlights the problems of sin and the worship of false gods. To make this more vivid, he introduced the story of Hagar and Sarah from Genesis as an allegory, so at the same time teaching the people more of the Old Testament Scriptures.

SLAVERY AND FREEDOM CANNOT CO-EXIST

Verse 21 is important as it addresses the basis of the problems that the Galatians were facing: *'you who desire to be subject to the law.'*

By putting their faith in Christ they had been given the most wonderful freedom. Did they now want to go backwards and put themselves under the Law? As Gentiles, they had never been subject to the Law and in their Christian walk this would be a backward step. Slavery to the Law, and freedom through God's grace, cannot co-exist. Paul was urgent in his hope that they would not take this step.

Paul used the story of Hagar and Sarah as an illustration that would highlight his opposition to imposing the Law on believers in Christ and especially on these Gentile Galatians. In it he plays on the different meanings of the word, 'law:'

1. The Law can mean the commandments that God gave to Moses for His people.

2. The Law can also mean the first five Books of the Scriptures as a whole, the Pentateuch, as they are also known as the Law.

Paul pointed out the impossibility of obeying the Law given to Moses, in thought as well as in deed; it is only through God's forgiveness of our sins because of Jesus' sacrifice on the cross that we can be made holy and acceptable to a holy God. Believers, whether Jew or Gentile, if they wanted to revert to slavery to the Law were virtually turning their backs on God's grace, offered freely through the coming of Jesus who was *'born of a woman, born under the law'* (Galatians 4.4).

Knots and Burrs

My mother was a great admirer of C.H. Spurgeon who was a great preacher and I remember her telling me of an illustration he used.

1. **Knots**: One story was about the 'Knights of the Thimble,' who were advised to "Always put a knot in your thread." Here, Paul was doing just that; he was teaching these unruly Galatians, by providing them with a knot: something from their daily life that they all knew about and understood. This story about Hagar and Sarah would be a useful reminder for them.

2. **Burrs**: Elsewhere, I was told, Spurgeon used another allusion to daily life; in it he referred to illustrations like these as "burrs." Again, that is something that the people, used to walking the fields and hills around them, were familiar with. Burrs stick to clothing with obstinate tenacity. Spurgeon suggested that every sermon should include a burr that would remain long after the main theme of the sermon was forgotten. Paul hoped that the illustration he gave would stick in the Galatians' memory as a good reminder.

As well as teaching a story from the Scriptures, Paul used the history of Hagar and Sarah as an allegory; one that he hoped would become a knot or a troublesome burr, and help them to long remember the main point of his argument.

THE ALLEGORY

When Abraham and Sarah had a child through the serving woman Hagar, the son was named Ishmael and he was technically the firstborn. He represents the slave sons of Abraham and thus the enslaving Mosaic, or Sinaitic Covenant as it was made on Mount Sinai. Paul likened this Sinai Mountain in Roman Arabia, which included much of what is now modern Saudi Arabia, Jordan and southern Syria, to Jerusalem where the majority of people were still Jews who had not turned to Jesus and so the whole city appeared to be still enslaved to the Law (v. 25).

The point here that Paul hoped would stick like a burr in the Galatians' memory was that those among them who trusted in the Law were behaving like the children of slaves, not as the children of God that they had become. If the Law were trusted for salvation, it could only lead to bondage and slavery (4.21–24). Therefore, believers must not revert to attempting to keep the Law as a means of salvation; if they did, they could only return to slavery.

CONTRAST THIS STORY WITH THAT OF ISAAC

Paul continued his illustration with another story. Isaac, the son of Abraham and his wife Sarah, was the exact opposite; he was the result of God's promise that was miraculously fulfilled by God and so he represents the free sons of Abraham.[33]

"The other woman" in Paul's story is, of course, Abraham's wife Sarah. But in his allegory, Paul likened her to the New Jerusalem, the heavenly Jerusalem: *'But the Jerusalem above is free, for she is our mother'* (4.26). Just as Abraham's wife Sarah was the mother of Isaac, so the descendants of Abraham and Sarah were the children of the free woman. As children of the promise, they will not be slaves but free inheritors of eternal life in the New Jerusalem.

---

[33] *See* Gen 16-17, 21, Gal 3.7, 29

Further, in verse 26, Paul quoted Isaiah's prophecy (Isaiah 54.1) that is related to one of the Old Testament Covenants, God's promise of future everlasting peace.

The slave woman represented the old Covenant people of God who did not bring blessing to the world. Contrasted with this is the New Covenant in which God's people will be like a mother who will rear a growing and healthy people. His peace will be created through freedom from the Law that Christ's death and resurrection have brought.

THE ALLEGORY EXPLAINED
To be absolutely certain that the Galatians understand the importance of this allegory and what it means, Paul explained it clearly in verses 28 - 31. He began by calling them his brothers and sisters: *'Now you, ... like Isaac, are children of the promise'* (4.28). The Jews always remembered that they were God's chosen people and for Paul, born a Jew, to align himself with these unruly, changeable Celts could only come from the amazing change that had occurred in his own life through the grace of God.

In his explanation, Paul continued to pursue his line of thought, although the very first words were telling. Some translations give the words, *'Now we'* rather than *'Now you'* (4.28). I find the former translation preferable, as it suggests that Paul was aligning himself with these unruly but lovable Celts and recognizing them as Christian brothers and sisters. Together they were children, not by physical descent as Ishmael was, but they had been born like Isaac as a result of God's promise.

Paul continued to explain why the Galatians had found themselves in this predicament with the lure of the false teachers: the child of normal birth, Ishmael, despised and persecuted Isaac (*see* Genesis 21. 9) who was born according to God's promise, *'Just as at that time he who was born according to the flesh persecuted him who was born according to the Spirit, so also it is now'* (4.29*)*. This is the situation that the Galatians had found themselves facing with the Judaizing teachers: they had sought justification by their own human efforts in being tempted to follow the Law instead of trusting in God's promise of justification by faith.

Paul urged his readers to understand what was happening here. They must remain strong and drive away those who would have them enslaved to the Law. *'Cast out the slave woman and her son'* (4.30b) suggests the casting out of those who seek justification through obedience to the Law instead of through faith in Christ. They, and he, were children of the free woman and must grasp that freedom if they were to retain their inheritance.

INTERPRETING THE SCRIPTURES

Interpretation of the Scriptures in order to shed light on a current situation that is causing problems has been a practice all through the ages and just as Paul, and Jesus before him, and the prophets before Jesus, lived as humans on Earth, so we continue that tradition. This type of interpretation is known as Hermeneutics.

While we know that the Scriptures were written for a specific time, they are also timeless and can speak to us today in so many situations. Paul had studied the Scriptures deeply as a young Jew and knew them well. Now he asked the Galatians to do the same thing, to search the Scriptures; he wrote: *'But what does the scripture say'* (4.30a)?

He is teaching the Galatians to use the Scriptures as a guideline, as a way of finding out God's will for them. That is still the case. The Old Testament Scriptures, which were Paul's Bible, were not just a collection of ancient books telling the history (His Story) of God and his relationship with the Jews, they are there to help us until the end of time. This is borne out later in Paul's letter to

Timothy where he wrote: *'All Scripture is breathed out by God and profitable for teaching, for reproof, for correction, and for training in righteousness, that the man of God may be complete, equipped for every good work'* (2 Tim.3.16-17).

There are many who claim to be Christian, and even advocates of other religions and cults, who would try to pull us away from what we know are the promises of God, enticing us with what they suggest is a more comfortable and easier way of Christian living. However, this can also turn into a form of slavery to principles that were certainly not taught by Jesus. His promises are true and so precious.

Christ is the yardstick by which we must measure everything if we are to retain our freedom and live in the way that God intended for His people. I often think of some excellent advice I once heard and have never forgotten; perhaps it was a knot or a burr: 'Just stop and think: what would Jesus do in this situation?'

To Think About or Discuss

1. What evidence does Paul use to verify his idea that slavery and freedom cannot exist together?
   Can you think of any other examples in the Scriptures?

2. Which sermons have you heard recently that acted like a knot or burr so that vital points have remained in your memory?

   - What was the effect of that recollection?
   - Why have you remembered it?

3. Think about the passage,
   'All Scripture is breathed out by God and profitable for teaching, for reproof, for correction, and for training in righteousness, that the man of God may be complete, equipped for every good work' (2 Tim. 3. 16 - 17).

   Discuss it, using some verses that you have found profitable and applicable to our lives in the twenty-first century.

≈20≈

CHRIST HAS SET US FREE
CHAPTER 5. 1 - 6

5 *¹For freedom Christ has set us free; stand firm therefore, and do not submit again to a yoke of slavery. ²Look: I Paul, say to you that if you accept circumcision, Christ will be of no advantage to you. ³I testify again to every man who accepts circumcision that he is obligated to keep the whole law. ⁴You are severed from Christ, you who would be justified by the law; you have fallen away from grace. ⁵For through the Spirit, by faith, we ourselves eagerly wait for the hope of righteousness. ⁶For in Christ Jesus neither circumcision nor uncircumcision counts for anything, but only faith working through love.*

In a brief but telling sentence Paul wrote that faith in Christ had liberated both him and the Galatians so they may take possession of true freedom and not be inveigled into succumbing to the yoke of slavery.

THE LAW AND SLAVERY
The yoke of slavery was the Old Testament Law. To submit to it meant virtual imprisonment. As we saw before, God's people did not always have the Law. Four hundred and thirty years after the Abrahamic Covenant, God gave the Israelites the Law through Moses (Galatians 3.17). It was a necessary step; the Law was God's way of teaching and His people learned from this, but they are human and therefore imperfect; they make mistakes and sin, and cannot by their own efforts remain holy.

The Children of Israel were rebellious. Frequently they were tempted away from worshipping God to making and worshipping idols; often they did not even attempt to live moral lives. The Law was a curse for them because it was impossible to obey, but it was important, as God's people needed a guide for pure living. However, it was not intended to be for ever. When Jesus came, through the sacrifice of His life God's chosen people could again become His children. Through Christ Christians have been liberated, set free from that slavery. Paul was very positive here. Then Paul's tone changed; he was still upset. The people he had shown the way to freedom and life had listened to new teachers who had brought old ways and ideas. They had spread their message that the way to be righteous, to be right with God, was to adhere to a whole plethora of Old Testament laws about food and circumcision. Paul was concerned. By following this teaching the Galatians were on the way to losing their newfound freedom. Paul exhorted his readers to be strong and stand firm against these imposters; they must not allow themselves to be ensnared into slavery.

These Celts prided themselves on being strong in body and in maintaining their cultural traditions, but Paul warned that if they acceded to the demands of these false teachers, they would surely become slaves, and that was something that these freedom loving people abhorred (5.1).

THE NATURE OF CHRISTIAN FREEDOM

Paul drove the point home in verse 2: if they turned to the Law for salvation, through circumcision, through this physical cutting, they would be taking on the mark of the Law. This would result in them cutting themselves off spiritually from the salvation that they had already grasped through Christ. By even contemplating such a step, these confused Galatians were showing that they did not completely trust Jesus. If they allowed themselves to be circumcised, these new Christians would be completely and surgically cutting themselves off from Christ. Righteousness through faith in Jesus would be annulled.

FAITH WORKS THROUGH LOVE

Paul reiterated that if they were circumcised, it would show that they desired to be justified through the Law: *'I testify again to every man who accepts circumcision that he is obligated to keep the whole law'* (5.3). But it is impossible to keep the whole Law, so they will fall from grace. No wonder some turned back to their old worship of idols.

As we have seen, the Law was not just the Ten Commandments, but it's even impossible to obey those. Remember Jesus warned that if we so much as think wrong thoughts, we break the Commandments [34] and defile ourselves. Jesus continued: *'That which comes out of a person is what defiles, for out of the hearts of men proceed evil thoughts.'* Jesus sums up the whole of the Law and the prophets in His *'Love the Lord your God with all your heart and with all your soul and with all your mind... You shall love your neighbor as yourself'* (Matthew 22.37-40). When we live and act in love, faith works through that love and there is no need for laws that confine and enslave. Through our faith we are free.

PRIDE GOES BEFORE A FALL

It's interesting to note that in the Old Testament we often find that if a great gift of grace is received, it almost always happens that it is followed by a great sin, and this is what is happening here. The Celts have been lifted up through grace and now they are likely to fall heavily if they do not heed Paul's warning.

It's not quite the same, but it might remind us of the saying: *'Pride goes before a fall,'* which is a paraphrase of Proverbs 11.2: *'When pride comes then comes disgrace.'* Elsewhere in the Old Testament Scriptures we read of where a promise or a blessing is followed by a big curse. There are many examples, but we can look at three.

---

[34] Mark 7.9-10

1. **Abraham**: When there was a famine, Abraham went to Egypt and was treated well because of his beautiful half-sister. She was taken into Pharaoh's house, but Sarah also happened to be Abraham's wife, and when Pharaoh discovered this they were sent away in disgrace (Genesis 12.10-20).

2. **Moses**: When Moses was with God on Mount Sinai and had received the Commandments, he came down with them only to find that in his absence his brother Aaron had sanctioned the making of a god of gold, a golden calf (Exodus 31.18 - 32.1-35), and God decreed that those involved would be blotted out of His book.

3. **David**: Even the great David, hero, psalmist and king, fell for Bathsheba. He ended up killing a man so he could steal his wife, earning God's displeasure (2 Samuel 11), and he was the best of the kings, except perhaps for Josiah.

I wonder if you have found that about pride, too. I certainly have. Pride can be a difficult sin to cope with and it's almost impossible to keep it under control without going to our Father God and asking for His help.

WAITING AND HOPING
Paul now returned to the Christian's eagerness to wait for righteousness, *'For through the Spirit, by faith, we ourselves eagerly wait for the hope of righteousness'* (5.5).

We do not try to produce perfect righteousness in our lives by our own efforts, because we cannot; it doesn't work that way. Instead, through living in the light and the power of the Holy Spirit and by faith in Christ we wait for God to complete our righteousness when we attain spiritual maturity in either our earthly death (Hebrews 12.23) or when Christ returns (1Corinthians 15.49).

This reminds me of the story of Ruth in the time of the Judges and how it can be applied to Galatians and to us. After having moved to a foreign land because of a drought, Naomi lost her husband and both her sons. At this stage, she was bitter; she had lost all hope for the future, all her dreams of grandchildren were gone. She decided to return to Israel. Perhaps the famine that had caused their move from their home in Bethlehem was now over. One daughter-in-law returned to her family, but the other, Ruth, while still mourning the loss of her husband, chose to accompany Naomi. Carrying all their earthly belongings, they walked all the way from Moab on the other side of the Dead Sea in what is now Jordan, back to Bethlehem.

Arriving home, their provisions and possibly their money had gone. Ruth, a foreigner, had to venture out in this new land to find food for them both. Moabites were the result of an incestuous relationship between Lot and his daughter, so Ruth was part Jewish, but only part, and a woman, and she knew she would not be welcome. However, an Israelite law helped: primary producers were to leave gleanings in their fields, such as barley that fell to the ground or grew around the edges of the field, or olives that had not fallen from the top of the tree. These were to be left for the poor.

Imagine the scene as she approaches, hungry and hoping. This may have been the first good harvest after the famine: the poor were hungry and they followed the workers, looking for what was left. As a foreigner, Ruth could only expect a negative response, so her experience is unexpected. God led her to Boaz' field. Boaz was a man of substance, he knew the Lord – and, as it later turns out, he was also Naomi's relative. Ruth was kindly given water, a precious commodity in that dry land, food, and there was plenty left for Mother-in-Law Naomi. Ruth gleans from early morning until sunset. She has garnered a whole ephah of barley! This is an extraordinary amount, about twenty-two litres, and enough to feed them for about two weeks.

Like God whom he worships, Boaz is an extravagant benefactor and Naomi recognizes that something special has happened. Such generosity is not human, it is from the Lord, and manifests His steadfast love. Her waiting and hoping was answered just as our waiting and hoping will be justified on the last day. It is God's gift through Jesus, regardless of sex, culture, or any other difference.

Neither circumcision nor uncircumcision count if we are in Christ; all that matters is faith working through love. Here Paul was dealing with the problem of externalism in religion (Galatians 6.5). This was strongly condemned by Jesus, too (Matthew 23). An unethical religion has no support from a gospel that is founded on the obedience and death of Christ. This outlook is not yet dead.

STANDING FIRM

Let us return to the beginning of chapter five: *'stand firm therefore, and do not submit again to a yoke of slavery (Galatians 5.1).'* It is just as important for us today to stand firm as it was for those long ago Celts. If we're tempted to adhere to Old Testament Law, and it is tempting because they are rules that we can live by. However, if we lock ourselves into them, we must obey them. Apart from the fact that Jesus pointed out that this was impossible, if we look at the Law spiritually, there are other traps. In our desire to trust and obey God's Laws we might become legalistic and tempted to tick off the boxes on a checklist. We think we know what God wants and act accordingly. Then our faith changes to complacency with our own performance and is watered down so that it has little to do with loving God or our neighbour.

On the other hand, if we have accepted Christ into our lives and have been freed from the constrictions of the Law, we may feel we can live however we choose. That is unacceptable. If we have given our life to God, it is no longer ours and we need to develop a relationship with Him so we are aware of the path He has chosen for us. We may be assured that the Law is of the Old Covenant and our way ahead has cast off that restrictive garment; it is now irrelevant. We have put on the New Covenant and are a 'new creation;' we are people living by faith in Christ in the power of the Holy Spirit. God promised righteousness, and although we're not there yet – we're still *'practising Christians'* and not perfect – that promise will come.

We must wait for the fulfillment of the promise in hope - and love while we wait. Christ has set us free from the Law, slavery, the world, sin, the flesh and the devil. All that counts is faith in Christ, expressing itself in love.

Where does Christian living end? It is expressed in love. We have freedom to love and serve others. Since we have tfreedom, we must stand firm, remembering our freedom is constantly under threat. We should put effort into our service to maintain it and prevent our reverting to slavery.

THE GREATEST OF THESE IS LOVE

In 5.6 we read about *'faith working through love.'* We can rephrase this to read: *'the only thing that counts is faith working through love.'* What a perfect description Paul gives of the new life! Everything is encircled by love, but that circle does not confine, it signifies freedom. The power for work and for service is love. It was love that moved God to all His work in creation and redemption. It was love that enabled Christ as man to work and to suffer as He did. It is love that can inspire us with the power of a self-sacrifice that does not seek its own but is ready to live and die for others. It is love that gives us the patience that refuses to give up on those who are unthankful or hardened. It is love that reaches out and overcomes. Both in ourselves and in those whom we serve, love is the power for our service. Let us make Christ our model and pray to love as Christ loves us.

We can obtain the power for love through our faith. Faith roots itself in Christ Jesus, who is all love. Faith knows, even when we only see in the glass darkly and cannot fully comprehend. The wonderful gift that has been given into our hearts is the Holy Spirit who implants God's love there. Faith knows that there is a spring of love within that can well up into eternal life; it is a love that can cascade out from that spring as rivers of living water.

Our faith in Christ assures us that we can love, that we have God's power to love established within us; it is bestowed on us through His grace as part of our new nature. We can use that power to exercise and show love in the way that we can serve both God and our fellow human beings. However, before we can rejoice in our possession, love through the gift of God's grace, we must accept it, grasp it, hold it and share it. We can only keep it if we do share it. Love is an amazing blessing from our Heavenly Father and it is so essential to our achieving a healthy Christian life. Through the power of the Holy Spirit love can so invigorate and strengthen us that we are immersed, embraced in its deep, indescribable joy.

To Think About or Discuss

1 In what ways might we unintentionally take up the yoke of slavery?

2 If we have cut ourselves off from the saving love of Jesus, what steps can we take to restore our relationship with Him?

3 Discuss other occasions described in scripture where pride has gone before a fall. Has it ever happened to you?

4 We are told that we should love, but sometimes it is not easy. How can we find ways to do this?

≈21≈

SPIRITUAL HEALTH
CHAPTER 5. 7-15

Paul began this part of his letter by praising the Galatians because they had been travelling the Christian way so well.

5 *[7] You were running well; who hindered you from obeying the truth? [8] This persuasion is not from him who calls you. [9] A little leaven leavens the whole lump. [10] I have confidence in the Lord that you will take no other view, and the one who is troubling you will bear the penalty, whoever he is. [11] But if I, brothers, still preach circumcision, why am I still being persecuted? In that case the offence of the cross has been removed. [12] I wish those who unsettle you would emasculate themselves!*
[13] For you were called to freedom, brothers. Only do not use your freedom as an opportunity for the flesh, but through love serve one another. [14] For the whole law is fulfilled in one word: "You shall love your neighbor as yourself." [15] But if you bite and devour one another, watch out that you are not consumed by one another.

Paul used the analogy of running (verse 7), an activity that was common for these people who lived in the hills. Most still travelled by foot, as did Paul and his little missionary band. Messengers ran long distances in relays to carry communications from place to place. Physical fitness was important to both Paul and the Galatians.

THE IMPORTANCE OF SPIRITUAL FITNESS

Both the Greeks and the Romans had games and physical contests to keep themselves fit. Physical fitness was important to them, but Paul was pointing out that spiritual fitness was even more important. Possibly the Galatians had embraced Paul's message and had been spreading it further among their fellow Celts in other parts of Galatia further to the east.

They had been running well, but what had happened? They have failed to reach the goal that Paul set before them. He needed them to understand where it is coming from, so he asked them who it was that had prevented them from doing what they knew was right. Paul was well aware that humans are unable to meet God's demands through their own exertion. It is only through Christ that we can obtain the means of righteousness and the hope of forgiveness.

BACKSLIDING IS INSIDIOUS

This insidious way of thinking that had been brought by the misguided teachers was new for the Galatians and Paul pointed out that *'This persuasion is not from him who calls you'* (5.8); it was misleading and certainly not from God. He had invited them to live in freedom through Jesus Christ. Now they were backsliding.

These mistaken ideas had crept in. Possible they were just small, almost imperceptible references and hints at first, but they had expanded and grown until they had taken over the whole group: *'A little leaven leavens the whole lump'* (5.9). This metaphor is another that the people were familiar with in their everyday living. They knew and understood the power of yeast: how a little leaven will grow until it ferments the whole batch of dough. Likewise, a few itinerant Christian teachers with a small flaw in their beliefs had misled the whole group of Galatian churches.

AVOID WRONG PATHS

However, Paul assured the people that he trusted that when he had explained and they saw the problem clearly they would agree with him that circumcision was not the path to follow: *'I have confidence in the Lord that you will take no other view, and the one who is troubling you will bear the penalty'* (5.10). The responsibility of this wrong teaching would be on the shoulders of those who came.

If Paul had taught the Galatians that, in order to be saved, it was necessary to be circumcised, the whole point of Jesus' sacrifice on the cross would be invalidated. *'But if I, brothers, still preach circumcision, why am I still being persecuted? In that case the offence of the cross has been removed'* (5.11). Jesus' crucifixion reminds us that our efforts to be right with God outside of Christ are useless. Jesus is the only way. Paul did not know seem to know the identity of the false teachers, but he was sure that in the final reckoning they would be punished by God for misleading the Galatian converts.

I am reminded here of Adolph Hitler. He was born in Austria, but came with his dreams and ideals right in the middle of a very crucial time financially for the German people. It was the depths of the Great Depression and he was offering the nation a way out of it. He lifted the people's spirits and then when he had taken charge it was too late. The people just had to comply with his ideals, or die. In the end, he paid the penalty for virtually playing god, but not before many innocent people had paid for his misdeeds as well.

PAUL'S CUTTING REMARKS
Throughout his letter, Paul referred to cutting. Circumcision is done by cutting and in verse 7 Paul asks: *'Who cut you off so that you have not obeyed what you know to be the truth?'* He reached his climax with this thought in verse 12: *'I wish those who unsettle you would emasculate themselves!'* He was so angry that he wished these false teachers would castrate themselves. These are the coarsest words in the New Testament. The false

agitators were cutting these new Christians off from Christ, causing them to stumble and lose their faith.

It is the same today. So often we are buffeted with falsehoods and lies from our leaders in government and even in church. We hope and pray that things will change and be different, but if we don't try and put right things that we know are wrong, a little yeast will soon infect whole generations of Christians. Paul's words remind us that there are right and wrong ways in Christian living. We can build on the right, but only when we have eliminated the wrong. To do this is not a minor operation. When Christians choose to live in wrong ways it removes them from Christ. For these Celts and for us, too, something that seems to be as good as keeping the Law can lead away us from His freedom.

God has given us a spirit of discernment and we need to use it. We must be discerning and rebuke those who suggest that it is all right for us to stray from what is right, however subtly it is introduced. We must be alert, and where we find so-called Christian preachers teaching things that are contrary to what we know is right, we need to stand firm. Paul's wise words, written to the Galatians two thousand years ago, are still relevant for us today.

GOD'S LOVE AND HEALTH OR ANNIHILATION

Up to this point in Chapter Five, Paul had been discussing the nature of freedom. By the Galatians reverting back to following the Law, he warned that they would forfeit the grace of Jesus Christ and lose the freedom that faith in Him brings. This must not be lost through their turning to legalism.

Paul now reminded the Celts that through him they were called to freedom, but that is freedom from the Mosaic laws, which were represented for men by the procedure of circumcision.

A LIFE BASED ON LOVE

The Galatians were warned that their new freedom did not give a licence for lawless behaviour: *'do not use your freedom as an opportunity for the flesh'* (5.13a). Nor was it an excuse for them to continue to be selfish and follow their sinful desires and flout God's moral laws. Instead, their new life in Jesus was to be based on love: *'but through love serve one another'* (5.13b). It was imperative that everything they did should be done in love. Instead of choosing to become slaves to the Law, they should turn their backs on such suggestions and, instead, concentrate on serving and being thoughtful for one another's needs.

Here Paul was referring to the nature of Christian freedom. He reminded these Celts that: *'the whole law is fulfilled in one word'* (5.14a). We know what that 'word,' or statement, is, because it is so well known and we use it in the liturgy every Sunday in the services: Jesus summed up the whole Law concerning our human relationships in one brief sentence: *'You shall love your neighbor as yourself'* (5.14b). This is a quote from Leviticus: *'Love your neighbor as yourself'* (Leviticus 19.18). Is Paul quoting from Leviticus here, or is this the single instance in the *Letter of Paul to the Galatians* where he has quoted the words of Jesus?

This 'word' is important for us, today, too. Through faith in Christ we are set free from all the things that would shackle us and hold us back. However, we need to remember that with that great gift of freedom comes a responsibility to fulfill God's desires for us and live in the way that He would have us live.

One of the important writings of Martin Luther, that great leader of the Reformation, included his *About the Freedom of a Christian.* His doctrine of salvation included the goal of complete union with Christ by means of the Word through faith. Although Jesus Christ came as God's Son, he came as a dutiful servant, and He came in love. We are to model ourselves on Jesus and serve one another with love. Love paves the pathway of freedom.

For Christians, the whole Law is summed up in only one commandment. When we obey that law and live as Christ intended, the entire Law is fulfilled in us and through us. This is the Law of the New Covenant: to love our neighbour – and ourselves.

LOVING OUR NEIGHBOUR
Thinking back to the story of Boaz, we may remember that he recognized the needs of a foreign woman, as his own mother had been. Those who love God can have nothing to do with racism, we accept and love God and He accepts and loves us, no matter what our nationality or colour. Boaz's thoughtfulness for Ruth and Naomi reflected the heart of God as he showed his love for his neighbour.

We can look at Boaz as a metaphor for God's great love. We Christians can know God even more deeply than Boaz did, because of how He showed His extravagant love for His people through allowing Jesus to die on the Cross for the expiation of our sins; accepting that sacrifice is the only way we can make amends for the guilt that our sins cause. We see His love in all our lives, in our families and in our church family. Through accepting His grace we are so blessed.

The marks of Jesus show in the lives of those who love God, as we show our love for our neighbour by helping the refugee, the poor, and the isolated. When we were slaves to the world, we were poor, but when we accept His love we became rich indeed.

When we become Christians we need to remodel our lives and be like Jesus, remembering that wherever we are is our mission field where we can share God's love and richness in mercy. Anyone we meet or who needs our loving help is our neighbour. Through faith in Jesus we are released from bondage and made both free to love and free to share in sacrifice for His sake. To love as He has loved us is our aim and ideal.

LOVING OURSELVES

Why not? We should not love ourselves in a self-centred way, but we have been created by God - and in His image. That's special and it follows that we should look after such a gift.

GOD'S TEMPLE

In John 2.19 Jesus referred to His own body as a temple and later Paul, in his first letter to the Corinthians wrote: *'Do you not know that you are God's temple and God's Spirit dwells in you? ...God's temple is holy, and you are that temple'* (1 Corinthians 3.16-17).

When we give ourselves to God, it is the whole of ourselves: body, mind and spirit. Many years ago when I was in the final year of school, our Principal, Dr. A. H. Wood, led our weekly Scripture classes. On one occasion that I have never forgotten, he introduced a term that was new to me: it was *self-abnegation*, the act of giving up something that is valuable. He was referring to giving up the whole of ourselves to God. Then we become His temple. How important is that temple to our spiritual health? How should we maintain it?

RESPECT GOD'S TEMPLE

Respect and cleanliness are important. Jesus said that it is what comes out of us that can defile, so we need to keep our interior, our thoughts and words, clean as well as our exterior, our bodies.

CARE FOR GOD'S TEMPLE
If we are responsible for caring for something that belongs to God and that He values, then we need to take the best care of it that we can at each stage of life. Much is written about it in the Scriptures, and we can find some words of wisdom in Ecclesiastes.

- The Spirit: *'Remember your Creator in the days of your youth'* (Ecclesiastes 12.1).

- The Mind: *'The words of the wise heard in quiet are better than the shouting of a ruler among fools'* (Ecclesiastes 9.17).

- The Body: *'The years draw near ... the keepers of the house tremble ... the grinders cease ... the windows are dimmed ... the almond tree blossoms ... and desire fails'* (Ecclesiastes 12.1, 3, 5).

DECORATING THE TEMPLE
We are warned that *'youth and the dawn of life are vanity'* (Ecclesiastes11.10). Beware of vanity and over decorating. In Peter's first letter, he wrote: *'Do not let your adorning be external... but let [it] be the hidden person of the heart with the imperishable beauty of a gentle and quiet spirit'* (1 Peter 3.3-4), and again in 1. Timothy 2.9: *'Women should adorn themselves in respectable apparel, with modesty and self-control.'* I should think that goes for men, too.

Further, we read in Leviticus 19.28: *'You shall not make any cuts on your body for the dead or tattoo yourselves: I am the LORD.'* I wonder what Peter and Paul would have to say about all the bracelets, chains, piercings and tattoos that we often see today? People see us as Christians and judge us accordingly, so we do need to be thoughtful about the way we present ourselves. Could tattoos look like graffiti on the walls of the temple? God made us the way we are and pronounced it very good. Do these decorations glorify His temple?

PETTY SQUABBLES AND GOSSIP

Paul warned the Galatians to avoid squabbling between themselves and causing enmity with idle gossip: *'But if you bite and devour one another, watch out that you are not consumed by one another'* (Galatians 5.15). Bite and devour one another! These Celts were often pretty good at that, and we can be, too, if we're not on the alert.

There were two brothers who always seemed to be at odds with each other, fighting and saying things that hurt the other deeply. Neither felt that they could forgive what had passed between them and their parents were at their wits end to know how to deal with it. It was poisoning the life of the whole family. The parents contacted a counsellor and tried to get the boys to go there to have their differences sorted out, but they refused. However, as a Christian family, they remembered that there is a Mediator, Jesus Christ. To go together to Him, humbly and in prayer in the quiet of their own home was not easy, but eventually they came to Him as a family, asked for forgiveness and received it both from the Lord and from each other and the rift was healed.

This warning from Paul is very timely for us, too. We can so easily get mixed up in all sorts of strife and troubles, and then it's not so easy to extricate ourselves again. Whether it's a family situation, a church group, a Bible Study, or any other group in the secular world, the consequences remain the same. Where people bite and devour one another, eventually the fellowship is likely to fall apart because it is no longer a fellowship.

To Think About or Discuss

1   Why is spiritual fitness important?

2   Who are my neighbours and in what ways can I show my love for them? What agencies does our church have in place that could help with this?

3   How can we love ourselves without becoming self-centred? How can this be compatible with self-abnegation?

4   Discuss strategies that we can use to extricate ourselves from trouble and strife and avoid disrupting a fellowship?

≈22≈

LED BY THE SPIRIT
CHAPTER 5. 16 - 18

5 [16] *But I say, walk by the Spirit, and you will not gratify the desires of the flesh.* [17] *For the desires of the flesh are against the Spirit, and the desires of the Spirit are against the flesh, for these are opposed to each other, to keep you from doing the things you want to do.* [18] *But if you are led by the Spirit, you are not under the law.*

In verses 13-14 Paul showed the Galatians the two sides of a coin by comparing the flesh and love. Now he contrasts the flesh with the Spirit presenting evidence to show them that to obtain holiness, Christians must hold fast to the freedom Christ gives. This remains relevant for us today.

THE DESIRES OF THE FLESH
The only way to overcome the desires of the flesh is to yield to the Spirit. Paul referred to strong bodily yearnings and the appetites of fallen humanity. We know how easy it is to long deeply for something that will not be good for us. It is so easy to develop bad habits, they almost happen by themselves, but are so difficult to break. How easy it is to self-indulge and to gratify the desires of the flesh! Whether it is the desire to satisfy strong sexual feelings for someone, the urgent beckoning of the pokies, over-indulging in alcohol, or merely wanting just one more (and then one more) chocolate, these desires of the flesh can be so difficult for us to deal with and overcome on our own.

But there is a way out. As Paul used stories as examples, there's a story told by an old soldier:

"When I enlisted, after passing the medical we all went to live in the barracks. Each day we had drill and some hard work, but there was plenty of time for fun. We often went to the local pub and a few drinks helped us to sing in the karaoke bar and mess around with other blokes. Then we were told we would be relocating to another State and we got some home leave. We had a great last night party and drank a lot. In fact, I got so drunk that I lay down in the middle of the road and could have been run over by some hooligan, if my mate hadn't pulled me back in time. You know, if I'd died that night, I'd have wakened up in hell. All I was interested in was *me* and having a good time.

"Well, we settled into our new quarters and soon did the rounds of all the pubs in the town, as well as discovering the nightclubs. One night we visited a brothel. It was so sleazy that I was disgusted and got myself out again. God must have been looking out for me that night, but I kept on drinking most nights until I was plastered. Soon we ran out of cash but had to do something, so we thought for a laugh we'd go to a 'Tea Meeting' at the church. The tea wasn't bad, some nice cakes and stuff. We thought we'd leave after that but the women were nice so it was difficult without being rude. Then most nights we went but I didn't listen much, except when she said they were praying for us. One woman asked if we'd help with decorations for a Christmas party for the down-and-outs. We did and then stayed and helped with the party, so I didn't even manage a drink at Christmas! What a turn around!

"A few evenings later that woman talked with me and told me Jesus died for my sins. That night when I went back to the barracks, I knelt down by my bed and gave my life to Jesus. I didn't care that some of the blokes were awake and saw. The next day, some of them came to congratulate me. I didn't understand it much when they said that I'd been led by the Holy Spirit, but I know more about that now."

THE SPIRIT LED LIFE
If we allow ourselves to be led by the Spirit, like that soldier we can break free from our cravings, the desires of

the flesh. When we invite the Holy Spirit into our lives He guides us in a personal way. Then we are freed and filled with the power of the Holy Spirit. This enables us to serve God and our fellow Christians in the way God has planned.

As freed people, we are released from the constraints of the Law; we are no longer 'under the Law' but under God's grace, and the activity of the Spirit is ongoing in our lives when we allow that to happen. Like most of us, the Galatians were Gentiles and so were not under the Law and never had been. Through the leading of the Spirit they should now live under a new law, the Law of Christ, which will provide for them a wonderful new life in God's love.

We, too, are no longer under the pre-Christian times and, through faith in Jesus, we are now to be led by the Spirit when we choose to follow God's path of freedom. He has given us the freedom to make decisions and choices, but we need to do these things with the guidance of the Holy Spirit. In that way we can receive spiritual power that will help us to use our freedom in the right way.

We must not abuse this freedom. Like the Galatians, if we choose to live under the Law, it will express itself in the works of the flesh and achieve only negative results that are almost impossible to overcome in our own strength. When we are led by the Spirit, the works of the flesh are overcome and replaced with works of the Spirit and so enabled to bear fruits of the Spirit that are pleasing to God.

TRANSFORMED BY THE GRACE OF GOD
The Galatians had never lived under the Law but now they were being tempted to do that by these preachers. Paul pointed out that the way ahead is to be totally transformed and to walk by the Spirit, enjoyed through God's grace.
As new Christians converted by Paul and his missionary team, the Galatians had been transformed. They were given a great gift: the wonderful opportunity through God's grace

to live by the Spirit and to be led by the Spirit. But it's so easy to be tempted, seduced to backslide. However, if they changed to desiring to live under the Law, which they have never done before, Paul warned that this would be a truly retrograde step. Instead of journeying forward together, they would find themselves being pulled in two opposite directions and would make no progress whatsoever in their Christian walk, but only travel backwards.

THE LAW HIGHLIGHTS OUR SINFUL NATURE

Paul went on to point out fifteen works of the flesh that the Galatians could be tempted to desire and seek to satisfy if they followed the Law. To do so would lead them to succumb to their sinful nature and bring to the fore in their minds the sins they committed before becoming Christians.

It seems that Paul was directly referring to a number of the wise saying in Proverbs. He warned that if the Celts chose to live under the Law they would be turning their backs on the wonderful transformation that occurred when they originally chose to allow their lives to be led by the Spirit.

To Think About or Discuss

1. What strategies can we use to overcome the desires of the flesh?

2. How can we overcome bad habits?
   Can we do it in our own strength?

3. What are the signs of a spirit filled life and how can we achieve this?
   Is it everlasting, or do we continually need to be filled afresh by the Spirit?

≈23≈

THE WORKS OF THE FLESH - 1
CHAPTER 5. 19-20a

5 [19]Now the works of the flesh are evident: sexual immorality, impurity, sensuality, [20]idolatry, sorcery, enmity, strife.

This list may remind us of the words of someone who came much later than Paul: Pope Gregory. Around 590 A.D. he named the Seven Deadly Sins as wrath, greed, envy, sloth, pride, gluttony and lust. Surely he must have based these on these words of Paul to the Galatians.

It must have been a time of revival in the Western world, as a history book I once taught from cited 597 A.D. as the time when Christianity first came to Britain, although actually it was there and had been since the time of Roman Britain. It is true that at this time Pope Gregory sent St. Augustine to Britain on a mission from Rome. It was Augustine who converted King Aethelbert of Kent to Christianity. Augustine also coined the famous words when he saw the fair-haired, fair skinned Angles' children: '*non Anglia, sed angelia*,' not Angles, but Angels.

However, the year St. Augustine landed in Britain was the same year that St. Columba died after his team had taken Christianity from Ireland to Iona and all along the Celtic west coast of Britain. About a century and a half earlier, in the 400s St. Patrick had taken Christianity from Scotland to Ireland! We need revivals and reminders from time to time.

SIN CUTS US OFF FROM GOD
The Law actually directs our attention to the sins of the flesh, it makes us think about them and arouses our sinful passions; to dwell on the Torah will not lead to inheriting

the kingdom of God, to life, but only to the works of the flesh and death. Paul stressed that *'those who do such things will not inherit the kingdom of God'* (Galatians 5.21). He emphasized the *doing* of these things; when we do these things we will not be fit for the Kingdom. Notice that he used the word '*do;*' we all fall short. Eternal life is not to be found in doing the Law, but in Jesus Christ who fulfilled the Law; those who are 'in Christ' also fulfill the Law, rather than obey it.

The Kingdom of God is a future inheritance, but it was also in the present for these new Christians if they did not turn aside and desert the pathway that they had chosen, the path of faith that leads to righteousness and peace. For the newly created Christians the new life is in the Spirit through union with Christ. These Christians had become a totally new variety of humanity and all the works of the flesh as enumerated in the Law were now put behind them. Like Lot as he fled with his family, they must not look back, only forward, or they could remain rooted to the spot as his wife who disobeyed, and so was unable to grasp the wonderful life ahead.

WICKED CRAVINGS AND ACTIONS

In verses 19-20a, Paul began to set out the works of the flesh. Without the transforming work of the Holy Spirit, sinful humans can succumb to wicked cravings and immoral actions and these Celts knew this only too well. It seems that in the time that Paul stayed with the Galatians he came to understand them well, too.

Let's look a little more at these works and see them for what they are. When we yield to such temptations we cut ourselves off from our Heavenly Father, who is so holy and pure. There can be no true fellowship with Him if we continue to retain any of these. To examine each one, not to dwell on them or gloat over them, can help build awareness. An understanding of them can safeguard against sin and help to avoid the temptation trap.

Paul must have known the Book of Proverbs very well and in this section I see again and again quotations that must have come to his mind. Proverbs 1.17 warns us against having too simplistic an approach to sin, as it can be a sign of spiritual laziness. Later, the compiler of Proverbs warns against laziness: *'Go to the ant, O sluggard: consider her ways, and be wise'* (Proverbs 6.6). There may be thousands of ants in a colony, but they all work together and use their energy to help the whole community. There is no place for laziness, only for wisdom, initiative and discipline.

Certainly, as Christians we like to think that we are uncomplicated and free, unrestricted by difficult rules, but God gave us brains and we should use them. We need to be aware so that we do not sin through unthinking ignorance. God created us to be thinking people and He expects us to use the mental powers that He has given us to assess situations and understand the consequences of choosing to sin. To keep ourselves holy, to ensure our personal purity, we need to avoid putting ourselves in compromising situations, such as the ones that Paul lists here.

1. SEXUAL IMMORALITY

This is referred to as 'fornication' in some translations. It means having sex when the man and woman are not married. I guess the temptation has been there since there have been men and women, and the Celts were not immune. They were Gentiles, as was the woman Jesus spoke to at the well. The temptation to jump the gun is still there for Christians when they are courting and today there are so many who are telling us that 'trial marriage' and simply living together are the norm. Abstaining until marriage can be a stressful time, but how wonderful when the couple is strong enough to wait, and what joy it is then!

Sex is a precious gift from God for both husband and wife. When it is abused it can also have highly destructive consequences. Later Paul was to write (1Corinthians 6.18) that every other sin is committed outside the body, but when a person sins against his own body, created in the likeness of Christ, a spiritual component is added to the equation, making sexual immorality doubly abhorrent.

Prostitution and adultery describe the sexual activity of a married man or woman with another outside the marriage. Although Paul, as a Christian, was now free from the Law, he understood the Law very well and would have been conversant with all the Books of the Old Testament. Again, in the Book of Proverbs, 6.26, we are told that in those days being with a prostitute cost about the same as a loaf of bread – it was cheap. The one who behaves in this way cheapens himself in his own eyes and in the eyes of God, but the man who has an affair with a married woman (and the same goes for a woman who has an affair with a married man) commits adultery and can lose his life. The writer asks so vividly, *'Can a man carry fire next to his chest and his clothes not be burned'* (Proverbs 6.27)? It leads to disaster and he causes his own destruction.

2. IMPURITY

Among the ways that Paul warned the Galatians that they may allow impurity to enter their lives is the telling of lies and revelling in dirty jokes. There is really no such thing as a 'little white lie'; a lie is an untruth and it is definitely not white and pure whichever way you look at it.

I love Jesus' description of Nathaniel's character: *'Behold, an Israelite indeed, in whom there is no guile'* (John 1.47). Oh, wow! How wonderful it would be to hear our Lord say that about us! No dishonest or devious behaviour. That would include the telling and revelling in dirty jokes. I'm sure the Galatians were quite good at these when sitting around a fire in the evenings.

It's friendly and fun, and good to laugh together, but we need to monitor what we laugh about if we're to keep our minds pure. What do we do when listening to a tale and then realize where it is going? Stay there and laugh at the end? Listen but try to keep a straight face? Or get up and walk away? It's not easy and we may need the power of the Holy Spirit to have the courage to walk away or comment on the fact that you don't enjoy dirty jokes.

3. SENSUALITY

Paul knew these Galatians. Living with them on a daily basis he had the opportunity to observe their behaviour and to note that before they heard his message they had lived in a very undisciplined way, doing anything they wanted, instead of following God's way. It was part of their culture and involved physicality, seductiveness and eroticism. Some was connected with the pagan temple.

These Celts were now struggling to correct such desires of the flesh, but with the influence of false preachers offering other ideas from what Paul had taught, it wasn't easy. They needed to take to heart Proverbs 6.23: '*The reproofs of discipline are the way of life.*' Every person is responsible for his or her own behaviour and the way of life should be guided by self-discipline.

4. IDOLATRY

Both idolatry and sorcery are ways to access evil spiritual beings. Such powers of darkness do exist, but we are to have nothing to do with them. For the Galatians, idolatry included worshipping the heathen gods of the people of other nationalities who lived near them, as well as their own gods. With these gods came many practices that were definitely unchristian, including the allure of temple prostitutes.

We, too, can be guilty of resorting to worship of idols. This means that if we worship anything other than Almighty God we reject the way in which God says He should be worshipped. It may be a football team, a shiny motorcycle, or that 'must have' for the home. Remember that Jesus said: *'I am the way, the truth and the life, no-one comes to the Father except through me'* (John 14.6). No one.

5. SORCERY

Sorcery is, of course, the practicing of magic, the use of it to tell the future, and being involved in witchcraft and superstition. Before the visit of Paul and his missionary team, the Galatians had participated in this, too.

While we may think, 'Well, of course I wouldn't take part in something like that,' what about those 'Stars' in your favourite magazine, fortune telling, or palm reading as a bit of holiday fun? What about Ouija boards that appeared in the U.S.A. around the middle of the nineteenth century? At that time they were thought to be compatible with churchgoing. They're still around and sometimes children even take them to school to share with their friends. Are they from God? Or are they the tool of the devil?

Sorcery and magic are on the rise. Just look at the number of references on the Internet. When we were living in the Dandenong Ranges east of Melbourne, we found we needed to lock the church. We could no longer leave it open for private prayer as various modern day witches and warlocks would come and steal the candles and other things for their own ceremonies.

6. ENMITY

The Galatians were always fighting with their neighbours, for the Romans, against Romans as mercenaries, and with each other. They were not above changing sides in the many wars and fighting that took place. Instead of tilling the soil or settling down to animal husbandry, their main occupation was bearing down on their neighbours in raids, killing and stealing. They were an emotional people with strong hates and loves and often maintained grudges and bore ill will towards each other and their neighbours.

7. STRIFE

These Celts that Paul had taken to heart were always in conflict with each other, causing strife and whipping up discord among their relatives and friends. One of the Proverbs (26.21) that Paul must have had in mind at this time warns that *'As charcoal to hot embers and wood to fire, so is a quarrelsome man for kindling strife.'* Where there's smoke there's fire, and these folk were forever kindling strife in which they often burned themselves.

Since becoming Christians, causing strife was something the Galatians needed to work on and overcome. Rejecting each other destroys human relationships and they needed to learn to love each other, but with these preachers stirring them up, it was easy to fall back into old habits of enmity.

One way of causing strife is through idle gossip; it can be unnecessary talk about others behind their backs, or it can be intentionally malicious. Again, in Proverbs (26.22), we find *'The words of a whisperer are like delicious morsels; they go down into the inner parts of the body.'* Gossip is like something desired and sweet, but it goes to the depths of the heart and festers, causing change and upset.

I'm reminded of a quote that I once heard; it went like this: *'Great minds discuss great ideas, medium minds discuss medium events and small minds discuss other people.'*

We may not all have great minds, but we can discuss

- Great ideas or experiences, such as our Christian walk or even something that has gripped our imagination in the media.

- Medium events, such as the football results of the club that we support.

The thing we need to avoid like poison is gossiping about other people. If we hear others indulging in this we can either try to point out that destroying the character of others is unacceptable, divert the conversation to another topic, or, as a last resort simply walk away and have nothing to do with such conversations.

The list of the works of the flesh continues in the next chapter.

To Think About or Discuss

1. Why do we need revivals and reminders to keep us journeying along the right path?

2. In the light of Proverbs 6.6, how can Christians remain vigilant against the works of the flesh?

3. Discuss each of these works of the flesh.
    - Are they applicable to us in the world today?
    - Do we understand the difference between them?
    - Why do we need to be able to recognize each?

4. Do you think that these first seven sins of the flesh truly depict the way the Galatians lived before the visit of Paul and the other missionaries? Do these cover their sins or do we need to look at the rest of the fifteen that Paul set out for them? Why?

≈24≈

THE WORKS OF THE FLESH – 2
CHAPTER 5. 20b - 21

5 *²⁰ᵇJealousy, fits of anger, rivalries, dissensions, divisions, ²¹envy, drunkenness, orgies, and things like these. I warn you, as I warned before, that those who do such things will not inherit the kingdom of God.*

8. JEALOUSY

Being rather highly emotional as a race, the Galatians were likely to be envious of others' achievements and possessions. As we have seen, before the advent of Paul they solved that easily, they just organized raids and took what they wanted. This was no longer an option. Jealousy includes being resentfully suspicion of others' intentions, and they often were, but it would have been better for the Galatians on one historical occasion if they had been a little more suspicious of the motives of their hosts when the leaders were invited to a feast and then slaughtered.[35]

9. FITS OF ANGER

These Celts often had strong feelings of displeasure, resentment and rage, they could be bad tempered, and as we have seen, they were licentious and gave free rein to their feelings among themselves and with neighbours. We have sayings about anger, such as, 'venting my anger,' 'it made my blood boil!' or 'I just saw red!' Controlling our anger can be difficult for anyone, but I suspect it is even harder for us who have inherited those Celtic genes.

When I first gave my life to Jesus at the age of ten, managing my bad temper was a big problem. In some

---

[35] *See* Appendix I

situations, I just could not control my anger. I realized that this was not Jesus' way, and now I was born again it had to be overcome. When I got really mad about something, I did not even 'see red' I saw 'black!' Everything else blacked out and I vented my rage on everything or everyone. I can sympathize with others in this situation. One young man I knew later was so angry that one day he punched a hole in the door and then hit the floor with his fist so hard that he broke his thumb. It was a hard lesson, but perhaps it was the only way God could teach him to control his anger. He wisely learned the lesson and grew considerably in his Christian walk and now helps others with this problem.

In my case, an uncle suggested that I count slowly to ten (my age) before reacting. It helped and I learned to contain my anger better, but I was not really cured until a few years later when I read the advice to say aloud, 'Praise the Lord!' ten times. At first I thought this was not a good idea, as I should not involve the Lord in my problem, apart from praying about it. It seemed disloyal, even treacherous to our Heavenly King, but then, in desperation, I tried it – and it worked! For the first few times I said it, I was seething, but then as I continued, it softened and by the time I reached about the eighth time, I found I really *was* praising the Lord, and that He helped me overcome the problem. He understood and was really with me! Hallelujah!

In discussing the Commandment '*You shall not murder*' (Exodus 20.13), Jesus said '*everyone who is angry with his brother will be liable to judgment*' (Matthew 5.22). We should not even think it, let alone say "I could murder him!" even in jest. It is difficult to learn to control our anger, but we know that He understands and will be with us as we work to control this and other negative emotions.

10. RIVALRIES
Negatives attitudes like anger can lead to violent disputes, disagreements, and the breaking up of relationships.

Rivalry is another work of the flesh, where two people or groups compete for the same thing. Some translations have 'quarrel,' instead of 'rivalries,' but this seems to be different, although they are both works of the flesh.

There's a saying: *'to quarrel with your bread and butter.'* It conjures up a spoilt child displaying a bad temper by throwing its bread and butter on the ground and going hungry. It's counteractive to our own interests to snarl at the thing that procures our living. How wonderful it can be to build a good relationship with each other and with God.

11. DISSENTIONS
This may seem the same as quarrelling, but it includes the Galatians disagreeing with each other, with their leaders, and lacking in unity and cohesion. The proclivity to this is what was revealed in the Celtic churches' upset with the false teachers' message. Some agree with it while others disagree and so they lack unity and cannot reach a satisfactory conclusion. Paul was anxious that his letter would help them to find their way out of the dilemma.

12. DIVISIONS
The people knew about these, as the Romans divided combatants in the circus into classes and called these 'factions.' Each class was distinguished by its colour and the combatants strove against each other as entertainment. The meaning of the word was extended to apply to members of political parties.

Many church groups can be guilty of harbouring factions and divisions. The Galatians did it and many nations do, too. They form themselves into small groups that do not welcome others. It's great to be able to meet together with friends or other Christians with similar interests. However, these can develop into factions, or sects that may have unusual, unbiblical ideas and opinions and may even develop into heresies, if the people concerned don't take care. The good news is that if we're aware of it, we're probably on the way to preventing it from happening.

13. ENVY
At first, this may seem similar to jealousy, but it goes deeper. It means a hostile longing to possess others' positions and belongings. Some translations give '*murder*' instead of '*envy*', so as well as inferring hostile longing, it means that the urge to have that desired position or those possessions has so overtaken the person that murder is likely to be committed to accomplish the aim.

14. DRUNKENNESS
Drunkenness (Galatians 5.21) and orgies are examples of how people use God's good gifts in destructive and sinful ways. It involves drinking until intoxicated and going on drinking binges. In the Old Testament Scriptures, wine was associated with joy and celebration. Nehemiah, Ezra the priest and the Levites (Nehemiah 8.10), told the people to celebrate the reading of the Book of the Law by eating well, drinking sweet wine, and sharing these with the poor. In Psalm 104.15 we read of '*wine to gladden the heart of man.*' Wine was to be celebrated, not used to excess.

When abused, wine was seen as destructive. Proverbs (20.1), warns that wine is a mocker, strong drink a brawler, and whoever is led astray by it is not wise. Again (Prov. 23.31-32), the young man is told: "*Do not look at wine when it is red... In the end it bites like a serpent.*" Scripture condemns drunkenness: in Paul's letter to the Ephesians (5.18), he wrote, "*do not get drunk with wine, for that is debauchery, but be filled with the Spirit.*"

When we say someone 'drinks like a fish' we mean that he overdoes it. Many fish swim with their mouths open – in humans it's not a pretty sight. The custom of drinking someone's health probably began with the ancient Greeks and Romans as a way to wish the other person good health, but drunkenness is not conducive to good health.

15. ORGIES

This is a warning against having loud, drunken parties. Some translations use the word 'carousing,' from the Danish. Their large drinking cup is called a *rouse*; to rouse is to drink from a rouse; to carouse is to drink it all, in company. An orgy is a wild drunken party that involves sexual activity. We see too much of that today, including with teenagers during 'Schoolies Week.' No wonder many parents, who can't afford it, choose to take their children on cruises and expensive holidays to avoid those excesses.

Paul warned that these ways can become a pattern of life and lead to binge drinking. This is not the life style of the Christian. Such conduct indicates they are not born of God; that they are virtuous is all a mirage. Such people do not have the Holy Spirit within. They are not God's true children. If tempted, it may be best to abstain altogether.

UNIVERSAL SINS

How many of these sins can I confess? They're universal sins, but look at them from a Celtic point of view. What about seeing them from a Christian point of view? Jesus Christ said that even if we think of these things without actually doing them we are sinning, such as in the above section on anger. In that conversation, Jesus went on to say that *'whoever says, 'you fool!' will be liable to the hell of fire'* (Matthew 5.22). It is our thinking and motivation that counts. We come short of the ideal. We were created to create, but we're often guilty of being hot-headed; we get caught up in the heat of the moment and forge ahead without thinking about the consequences of succumbing to our desires and all we create is a mess of our own lives and sadly, sometimes the lives of others as well.

'Sins of the flesh' seems to be an old-fashioned concept that we don't use much these days, so we are likely to skip

over it, but what it stands for is important. Sins of the flesh are almost as old as humanity itself and are an ever-present temptation. So much of what we hear and see on the TV and internet every day could be categorized as 'sins of the flesh.' We become inured against feeling any repugnance. Beware of the world – be in it, but not of it. It has always been the same. The Psalmist so long ago asked,
'How can young people keep their way pure?
By guarding it according to your word' (Psalm 119.9).

God's Word is our guide and our guard for young and old and those in between as well.

My late husband had a story from our years on Papua New Guinea that he loved to tell. It was a conversation he had with a nurse who had been sent to him for discipline.
" Are you pregnant?" he asked.
"Little bit," was the reply.
However, she was either pregnant or not. There is no in-between. It's the same with sin. We often think things are comfortable in shades of grey, but when it comes to The Judgment, there is no grey, only black and white. It's either, Yes, or No. There can be no maybe.

SIN AND THE WORLD

Remembering Pope Gregory's Seven Deadly Sins, I heard it said recently that if we attempt to control these sins in our lives, we expose ourselves to many health problems. The world's remedy is a therapy that allows us to express our anger, greediness, and jealousy, 'destructotherapy.' This therapy provides ways for people to express their anger and learn to control it in special places where they can smash things such as computers, plates, and even cars.

Other sins are coped with through sublimation or changing the urge, as with greed, envy and slothfulness, by using it for good, changing greed to a desire to improve knowledge, slothfulness by using spare time wisely.

These suggestions are good, but for the Christian so is prayer and maintaining a good relationship with our Father. Then when problems arise we can allow Him to change our sinful desires so they can serve useful purpose in our lives.

ADVERSITY AND HOLINESS

Whaat is the connection between adversity and holiness? When adversity comes, it can reveal the corruption of our hearts. We don't know ourselves, and are not aware of the depths of sin and the possibility of sinning that remains in us until we meet with adversity. We study Scripture, agree with the teaching and assume that this means obedience. We intend to obey. We read that list of Christian virtues, the 'fruit of the spirit,' and agree that we want all those traits in our lives? We think we are making good progress in growing these fruit. Then adversity comes and we find we don't know ourselves at all. We are alarmed at our own reactions. God can use adversity to teach us how to become aware of our sinful nature and how to overcome it with the Holy Spirit's guidance, so we can work to eradicate our unholy desires and stubborn wills and become more like Jesus, more holy and acceptable to our Heavenly Father.

Yes, in many ways today we have a very different life-style from Paul and the Galatians. Think of our communication systems: they are almost instantaneous; the speedy ways we can travel, the variety of foods available in the local supermarket. But pause for a moment: basically we remain much the same inside – unless something happens that causes us to change our behaviour and attitudes. We live in the Twenty-first Century, but if we have Celtic ancestors our genes have their roots way back.

As Celts, we can go back aeons before these Gauls settled in the part of Turkey that came to be known as Galatia. Then Paul and his friends came and taught these heathen about Jesus. They rejoiced in their freedom from things that had chained them to a fearsome, sinful past. Belief in

Jesus set them free and they greatly embraced their new direction. That is, until the Jewish Christians came and confused them with a different message. For these teachers, the ancient Jewish Law had been their life and background and they understood their allegiance to Jesus in the light of this, but as was pointed out by Paul, faith in Jesus Christ was all that was necessary for redemption for Gentiles who did not have this heritage.

These 'works of the flesh' are the evil, negative characteristics that are brought to the forefront of our minds when we attempt to obey the whole of the Law. We need to be aware of them, but to dwell on them will only lead us in exactly the wrong direction. Instead, Paul contrasts them with the Fruits of the Spirit which are the ideal aims for living the believing Christian's new way of life.

To Think About or Discuss

1. Which of these final eight sins of the flesh do you think is the most difficult to identify and eradicate?

2. In your opinion, is merely thinking about one of these sins as bad as committing it?

3. Do you think that destructotherapy is the best way to overcome a sin such as anger? Will that sin be eradicated permanently from the person's life or are there alternative ways to do this?

4. What are the dangers of thinking about these sins of the flesh too much? What can we do about it?

≈25≈

THE FRUIT OF THE SPIRIT - 1
CHAPTER 5. 22

5 [22] *But the fruit of the Spirit is love, joy, peace, patience,*

THE NEW AGE OF THE SPIRIT
Paul now enumerates nine beautiful fruits of the Holy Spirit, contrasting them with the fifteen sins of the flesh. These fruits are the exact antithesis of what happens if we continue to choose to follow the Law.

Again we can see Paul's great depth of knowledge of the Scriptures; here he was drawing on Isaiah, a favourite of his and of many of us today, too. In several places, including Isaiah 32, we find that it was probably the basis for Paul's writing about these Fruit of the Spirit. They are the result of a new age of the Spirit that came with Jesus' death and resurrection and it replaces the old Laws that are no longer necessary.

As Paul pointed out so clearly, the Law cannot bear good fruit and if the Galatians lived by the Law of Moses and were committed to circumcision they would be unable to bear the good fruit that he wished so much for them to enjoy. However, if they lived by the Spirit and not by the Law, they will have true and eternal life. It is the same for us: it is only the presence of the Holy Spirit within us that can help us to accomplish this. There is no law against these beautiful fruit that point us to the way of holiness.

I love finding out where the words we use come from, as English is such an eclectic language and, as you will notice, these Fruits of the Spirit are all simple words that we use every day: Two are from Old French, three from Latin, three from Old English, and the final one is composed of both Old English and Old French words. All these nine words have deep meaning and have been absorbed into the English language and have been familiar to us for a long time.

1. LOVE

(Old English): This word suggests strong feelings of affection, attraction, pleasure and admiration. Love takes a central place in the Bible and is mentioned there 414 times. Paul placed it first in his list of fruits of the Spirit, as it is the most important. The old saying, *'Love makes the world go around'* sounds rather glib, but it's true!

There are many different types of love and here we find that English is a little lacking when compared with some other languages. Most of these words can be found in Greek. In English we need to add another word to qualify these differences, so we speak of things such as God's love,' 'our love for God,' 'brotherly love,' 'Christian love' and 'romantic love.' We can find all of these in the Bible.

- **God's Love for Humans**
  In the Old Testament we read of God's love for His chosen people. It is a 'steadfast love' (Exodus 20.6a); he us leads *'with the bands of love'* (Hosea 11.4). The prophets take up the theme: *'I have loved you with an everlasting love'* (Jeremiah 30.3).

  In the New Testament we learn from Jesus that God's love is for all people of every race and condition, and we see it in God's Fatherhood, His love for His children: *'God so loved the world that He gave His only Son, that whoever believes in Him should not perish but have eternal life'* (John 3.16). God loves us so much! Jesus also said, *'If anyone loves me, he will keep my word, and my Father will love him, and we will come to him and make our home with him'* (John. 14.23).

How amazing that our great God blesses us with His love!

- **Humans' Love for God**
  In the Ten Commandments we find that those who love God will be blessed by His steadfast love (Exodus 20.6b). Our love for God is so deeply expressed in the liturgy that we use each Sunday, as a prelude to the Confession and Absolution. It comes from Deuteronomy 6.5: *'You shall love the Lord your God with all your heart and with all your soul, and with all your strength.'* Jesus called this the *'great and first commandment'* (Matthew 22.38); but He added, *'with all your mind'* (Matthew 22.37). In early Hebrew thinking the word 'heart' included 'mind,' but by Jesus' time, they were seen as two separate concepts.

- **Brotherly love**
  The Greeks call this *phillia*. We have a beautiful example of brotherly love in the story of David and Jonathan (2 Samuel 1.26). In His conversation with the lawyer, Jesus' summary of the Ten Commandments includes love of our neighbour: *'You shall love your neighbour as yourself'* (Matthew 22.39). We should love our brothers and sisters in Christ as much as we love ourselves.

- **Agape**
  In the Bible, we often read of the word, 'charity.' This is a translation of the Greek word, *Agape*, and we often use it now, as it is the best way to describe it. Agape refers to the love that continues to care, whatever the circumstances. It is also sometimes known as 'Christian love.' It is our responsibility as Christians; John reminds us of

this: '*If anyone has the world's goods and sees his brother in need, yet closes his heart against him, how does God's love abide in him*' (1 John. 3.17)?

Agape is sacrificial love that comes from God and we see it in the love that Jesus had for the world. It covers the service we can do in working for charities, but it is much more. It is everywhere a kindness is done, but it is also rare. James (2.8) even went so far as to call it '*The royal law*.' It is the Law of Christ the King and is to be obeyed by all who count themselves as His subjects.

- **Romantic love.**
  The Greek word for this is *Eros*. The Bible has much to say about the love between a woman and a man. We read of the deep and lasting love of Jacob for Rachel, how he worked for her father for seven years, but they only seemed like a few days '*because of the love he had for her*' (Genesis 29.20), and then he was deceived and had to work for another seven years. That's devotion!

  In the Song of Solomon, we read that '*his banner over me was love*' (2.4). This beautiful Song is full of wonderful endearments, such as the woman's dream when she longs for her lover and eventually finds him, leading to a moment of intimate tenderness. God created us to enjoy the delight of sexual pleasure within marriage and it is sad to see how it is often perverted with trafficking, pornography and sexual abuse.

2. JOY

The word originally came from the Old French and to us it means great pleasure and happiness, but it is deep and means so much more than happiness. The letters of J-O-Y have often been referred to as an acronym for Jesus,

Others, Yourself. It suggests that if we think of Jesus first in our lives, then of others and lastly of ourselves, we will achieve lasting joy. It's not original, but I love that thought and it fills me with gladness that this is a simple motto, but one that we can follow all our lives until we reach everlasting joy in His Kingdom.

The Psalmist reminds us to *'Be glad in the Lord, and rejoice, O righteous, and shout for joy, all you upright in heart'* (Psalm 32.11)!

- **The joys of Mary**
  When we think of Mary, we remember she was so young when she became pregnant and we can imagine the pains that must have pierced her heart to see her first-born Son endure such undeserved suffering for the sake of the world. But sometimes we refer to the joy that Mary must have also experienced as Mother of the earthly Jesus.

  The joys of Mary include the annunciation, the visitation, the nativity, the adoration of the three wise men, the presentation of Jesus in the temple, and the discovery of her young Son in the temple discussing the Scriptures with the learned doctors of the Law. These joys she would have treasured.

3. PEACE
Peace often seems to be elusive, both in the world as an absence of war, and in our spiritual lives as tranquility and God's peace in our hearts. The word comes from the Latin. In Proverbs 14.30 we read, *'A tranquil heart gives life to the flesh,'* and in Psalm 29.11: *'May the Lord bless his people with peace!'* Best of all are Jesus' words recorded by John: *'Peace I leave with you, my peace I give to you. Not as the world gives do I give to you'* (John. 14.27).

For a moment, let us think of "passing the peace" which many Christian denominations incorporate into the service of Holy Communion. It comes at a special place in the service, after the absolution, when we have made our peace with God. Then, with a handshake and possibly the words, *"Peace be with you,"* we make peace with our neighbour. By sharing God's peace with each other during the Eucharist, we are signifying our Christian unity.

> This word, 'peace' reminds me of my father's boat that my parents and I loved when I was quite small. Called *'The Pax,'* it was such a peaceful boat. When we boarded her, we seemed to leave all the worries of the world behind and enjoy the peace together. Dad would motor down the Yarra River and negotiate under Princes Bridge and the other bridges until we reached Port Phillip Bay.
>
> There would be the brief busyness of fiddling with ropes and pulleys as Dad got the sails up while Mother took the helm, then the engine was turned off and Dad took the helm. Mother would sit down with a happy sigh, and say, "Listen to the silence!" The sails billowed and the sea lapped the wooden sides of the boat as we gathered speed.
>
> Soon we'd be out in the centre of the Bay. Dad would let down the anchor, get out the fishing-lines while Mother beat up a batter. Then Dad lit the petrol pressure stove. Fish for tea, a sing-song of favourite hymns around the folding pedal organ and soon we would be gently rocked to sleep. *The Pax* and peace just seemed to go together.

When we have God's peace in our hearts it is not for ourselves alone; it is something that we can share with others, especially in the area of reconciliation, restoring friendly relations between people in our own family, our country and in nations overseas.

God's peace is such a beautiful fruit of the Spirit but frequently it seems to be quite absent in a stormy, rudderless world where wave after wave threatens, maybe in a person's heart, between couples and friends, between nations. We think of how Jesus calmed the waters and it can be the joy of Christians to try, with the power of the Holy Spirit to give us strength, to bring peace and calm to these troubled waters. Just this week we were mourning the passing, and celebrating the life, of Nelson Mandela. Although he was imprisoned for twenty-seven years for his stance against Apartheid in South Africa, yet he persevered and was able to bring about peacefully such great change in the country that he loved, and still forgive those who had caused him and many others such suffering.

4. PATIENCE

Patience is a fruit of the Spirit that can be elusive at times. In a world of deadlines, timetables, rush and bustle, people often expect everything to have been done yesterday. The world is not very patient and we find that Christian patience is something that we need to work on in our lives.

This word, patience, comes to us from Latin. It speaks to us of the ability to accept delay, troubles or suffering without becoming angry or upset. The noun 'patience' is not mentioned in the Old Testament, only as 'patient' and 'patiently,' but it is used thirty-seven times in the New Testament, as when Jesus explained the parable of the sower to His disciples, *'As for that in the good soil, they are those who hearing the word, hold it fast in an honest and good heart, and bear fruit with patience'* (Luke 8.15).

Patience was also the name of a herb that helped to relieve lepers' suffering, which was often very prolonged. Then there is the saying we probably learned in school:
> *"Patience is a virtue, possess it if you can;*
> *Seldom found in woman, and never found in man."*

That's not entirely true, I've known men who have been extremely patient when waiting on God. However, patience is something that we Christians often seem to need to learn. It appears to come naturally to some people, but for most of us mortals, we are always showing our impatience, wanting something to happen immediately, with that catchphrase:
'When do we want it? NOW!'

We're even impatient in our prayers. We pray to God, asking for something we think we desperately need, or asking for guidance in a special situation and we expect an instant answer. But the Lord of Eternity understands our needs. He also knows when it is good for us for our supplications to be granted and when it is better for us to wait for the right time.

God's timing is perfect and patience is a lesson that is not easy, but one that we need to work on as we learn to rely entirely on Him. Patience as a Fruit of the Spirit comes with an even temper and with forbearance. These can be difficult to acquire, so we need to pray to our Heavenly Father for guidance in this area of our lives.

To Think About or Discuss

1. What are the results of living in the Spirit? How can this be achieved?

2. Do you think that Paul had any particular reason for putting love as the first of his list of fruits of the Spirit?

3. Which of these four fruits have you found to be the most difficult to grow? Why?

≈26≈

THE FRUIT OF THE SPIRIT - 2
CHAPTER 5. 22b - 23

5. ^{22b}*kindness, goodness, faithfulness,* ^{23}*gentleness, and self-control: against such things there is no law.*

The following five Fruit of the Spirit complete the nine that Paul wrote about in his deep desire to help the Galatians to learn how to live the Christian life.

5. KINDNESS

The word 'kindness' comes from the Old English and I guess that kindness includes our being caring, friendly and generous. We can be kind to other people: those around us in our families, in our church community and those we meet every day in our workplace and travel, whether driving or commuting on public transport.

We need to be aware of the need for our generosity and kindness to those living in far away places where there is war, famine and destitution, both as individuals and as a nation. God's children suffer in many ways and Christians have a responsibility to show our kindness however we can: by praying, giving and encouraging our governments to give aid. Sometimes we are not aware of the great need for prayer for our neighbouring countries: a good source of information is to take notice of the News, whether it is by word of mouth, newspapers, radio, television, computer or whatever. Then we know where the most need for our actions and prayer lies.

Our Heavenly Father, of course, is our greatest example of kindness. In the Book of Ruth, Naomi praised both Boaz and God: 'May he be blessed by the Lord, whose kindness has not forsaken the living or the dead' (Ruth 2.20)! We read in Proverbs, in that famous passage about the good woman, *'She opens her mouth with wisdom, and the teaching of kindness is on her tongue'* (Proverbs 31.26).

Then we should be kind to the creatures in the wonderful natural environment that God has created; kindness to the animals and birds, those that are our pets, of course, but especially to those that are suffering because of the thoughtlessness of human beings and the way we destroy their environment for our own selfish ends.

6. GOODNESS

The Old English word, 'goodness,' means maintaining a high standard, of knowing the difference between right and wrong and our choice to be morally right. Goodness may also involve qualities such as politeness, obedience and benevolence. It is often connected with a word from the Latin that translates as 'generosity.' Goodness is suggestive of the quality of being noble and magnanimous.

One of the characteristics of God is His goodness to humankind. Nehemiah praised Him for His protection and goodness as the Israelites wandered in the wilderness and took possession of the Promised Land: *'So they ate and were filled and became fat and delighted themselves in your great goodness'* (Nehemiah 9.25).

- The minister at the church I attend preached a series some time ago on 'Values' in our lives and one he chose to discuss was 'Living Beyond Reproach.' Is that the reproach of our families, our neighbours and friends? We may manage to bear the fruit of goodness with them – or do we try to 'pull the wool over their eyes!' We can't do that with God. He knows our innermost being and what we are like in our hearts and minds.

Goodness, as a Fruit of the Spirit also means keeping oneself holy. Because of our human nature, we cannot be perfect while we live on this earth, but that is what we strive for, our aim. We need to keep ourselves as holy as possible for our Father so we can have fellowship with Him. He is all perfection and all goodness and we should try to model ourselves on His Son, Jesus, who came and lived on earth to show us the way. He did not sin and so is the perfect example of goodness and holy living.

7. FAITHFULNESS

This word means remaining loyal, true to the facts or to the original. It comes from the Latin and signifies complete trust or confidence in someone, or a strong belief in a religion. Faithfulness for me means both those things, being loyal to one's friends and especially one's husband, and, in Christian living being faithful to our Father God.

God is faithful to His children. In Psalm 40.10, David sang *'I have spoken of your faithfulness and your salvation.'* In the Book of Lamentations (3.23), the writer cries out, *'Great is your faithfulness.'* God's faithfulness to us is the greatest example we could possibly follow. The highest aim of faithfulness for the Christian is to have complete trust in our Lord Jesus Christ and a strong belief in God.

8. GENTLENESS

The word comes from Old French and suggests someone who is genteel, highborn and kind. There is no rough and violent behaviour, but only mildness, kindness, humility, meekness and courtesy. The Psalmist (18.35) praised God for His gentleness, *'Your gentleness made me great.'* God can be very gentle with us when necessary. Later, Paul wrote to the Corinthians (2. 10.1) about *'the meekness and gentleness of Christ.'*

Gentleness is not always valued today, but that is due to a misunderstanding. It does not imply that we should allow others to walk all over us, but that we are courteous and gentle in the way we handle situations, being thoughtful for the feelings of other people – and even animals – and that we deal with them gently in a kind and loving way.

9. SELF-CONTROL

The last of this wonderful list of Fruits of the Spirit is composed of two words: the first part of this concept, *self*, is an Old English word. It refers to a person's essential being, the individual personality that distinguishes him from other people. In psychological terms, we might think of it as *ego*, our sense of our own worth, the part of our mind that is responsible for the interpretation of reality and a sense of personal identity. This can be compared with our *id*, the essence of our self, the unconscious mind that consists of our basic inherited instincts, needs and feelings.

As Christians, we are not so interested in self. When we think of self, we often link it with 'centred;' and we know that being self-centred is not good, but rather, to be '*God-centred*' is our aim. Here, Paul links 'Self' with 'Control.' The notion of self-control infers restriction of something, a checking, a self-restraint, containing oneself successfully. Self-control includes the ability to control our emotions or behaviour in difficult situations. This is not easy and something that we, as Christians, often need to work on. For us as, whether or not we are Celtic, it seems to be one of the most difficult of the Fruit of the Spirit to attain.

It can be difficult to control ourselves; even in something simple like a conversation. How often something the other person says triggers off a similar situation in our own lives and we jump in with our own experience instead of quietly listening.

1 Firstly, this isn't polite. We should allow our friend to have her say. This doesn't sit so well with Celts, as they like to hold the floor and tell a good story in a dramatic fashion. When we were children, my Mother dealt with this by explaining that to hold a good conversation was like playing *ping-pong*. The other person sends us the ball and then we send it back again. We don't keep it for too long, or it isn't a good game. How wise!

2 Secondly, if we listen we may learn something that is good for us to know. Remember Jesus said, '*You who have ears to hear: listen*' (Mk. 4.9). Listening is important and it is a skill that needs to be worked on. Through learning to listen, God may use us to help other people, or we may even hear a message that is rfrom God. He can teach us much through the words of others; sometimes He even uses non-Christians to reach us.

FRUITS OF THE SPIRIT AND ADVERSITY

We can be sure that the development of a beautiful Christ-like character will not occur in our lives without adversity. Someone once wrote in my Autograph Book, '*May you have just enough clouds in your life to produce a beautiful sunset.*' Clouds are essential if we are to use those fruits and grow our characters.

Think again of those lovely graces that Paul calls the Fruit of the Spirit. The first four traits we looked at: love, joy, peace, and patience, can only develop as a result of adversity. We may think we have true Christian love, but then someone offends us or treats us unjustly. We begin to grow angry and resentful. We may conclude we have learned about genuine Christian joy until our lives are shattered by an unexpected calamity or a great disappointment. Adversity spoils our peace and tries our patience.

God uses those clouds, those difficulties to reveal our need to grow so that we reach out to Him to change us more and more into the likeness of His Son. Both Paul and James write about the need to continue to rejoice in our sufferings. Paul, in his letter to the Philippians, wrote, '*Rejoice in the Lord always; again I will say, rejoice*' (Phil. 4.4). Rejoice? Most of us have difficulty with that idea. We don't enjoy pain. But it can be beneficial. Through the expectation of the results our character can be built up, giving us cause to rejoice in adversity. We rejoice because we know that God is in control of those upsetting circumstances and He is at work through them for our ultimate good.

To Think About or Discuss

1. How can we grow these fruit in our lives? If we do work on them, how can they help us to grow to maturity as Christians?

2. Which of these five fruit do you find the most difficult to grow in your life? What do you find is the thing or event most likely to impede its growth?

3. Discuss the quote 'May you have just enough clouds in your life to produce a beautiful sunset.' Do you think that clouds in our lives can truly help to produce a beautiful sunset? What are our usual reactions to adversity?

≈27≈

GUIDED BY THE SPIRIT
CHAPTER 5. 24 - 26

5 [24] And those who belong to Christ Jesus have crucified the flesh with its passions and desires. [25] If we live by the Spirit, let us also keep in step with the Spirit. [26] Let us not become conceited, provoking one another, envying one another.

Several times in this letter Paul has warned that the Christian can be easily led astray from the right path. It is only through following the leading of the Holy Spirit day by day, that the Galatians could keep their feet on the right path. It was not easy for the Galatians, especially with their volatile Celtic background. It is the same for us: if we are to follow the path that God has planned for us, we need the guidance of the Holy Spirit, day by every single day.

BELONGING TO JESUS

Through the efforts of Paul and the mission team, these Celts made the decision to follow Christ and were baptized. Now Paul pointed out that *'those who belong to Christ Jesus'* will only be able to live the Christian life if they allow the Holy Spirit to guide them in all that they do. For a people whose culture had always thrown off submitting to authority, this is not easy for them. With their heathen religion that encouraged sexual passions and desires, as well as other deviant practices, this will require a great turn around in their lives. They may choose to do it, but carrying it through day by day will be quite a challenge.

When we choose to make that commitment to belong to Jesus, we must also submit to the crucifixion of *'the flesh with its passions and desires.'* Making the choice is only the beginning, there is so much more for us to meet, grapple with and overcome along the way. Our passions and desires can seem to keep cropping up at the most inopportune moments and we can find that, with all our high aspirations and intentions we are weak and powerless. That is where we need to remember that when we belong to Jesus we can *'live by the Spirit'* and draw the power we need from God's Holy Spirit.

ONE WAY

For everyone living on the planet, if they have received the invitation to the Christian faith, then belonging to Jesus can be part of travelling on the journey of life. Life is a great journey for all human beings, but it's entirely our choice as to the destination. God gives us the free choice. There are two ways to go, but only one that is worth choosing.

To put it another way, if we decide to fly with Jesus and be piloted by the Spirit, there is no other route we can possibly follow. It's a long journey and should last for the rest of our lives. There's no First Class, Business Class, or Economy, we are all equally in the one class. It's a one-way ticket and the price, which even the wealthiest person could not afford, has already been paid. He is the only way.

LEAVE THE OLD BAGGAGE BEHIND

If we are to belong to Jesus, then on this journey we need to *'have crucified the flesh with its passions and desires'* (Galatians 5.24). We need to cast all that old baggage into the incinerator and leave it well behind us.

How wonderful, and what a precious privilege it is to belong to Christ Jesus! We can joyfully sing songs about it and lift our hearts to Him along with our voices. Now we belong to Jesus! However, the business of crucifying the flesh with its passions and desires seems to be much more difficult, especially for people of Celtic origins. We often find ourselves relying on our emotions, our passions and desires rather than on objective reasoning. In Christianity there is a place for our emotions, God does not expect us to be without feeling. Jesus is our model and He experienced emotions during His life on earth: He showed anger, He was sad and wept, and He told jokes. It's the fleshly passions and desires that can lead us along the wrong path that Paul is condemning.

Yet again, Paul puts his finger right on the place where the problems can lie. And yet, if we truly belong to Jesus, this is what must occur. We must crucify the flesh and this can be something that we find we can't possibly do in our own strength. It can only happen through the power and guidance of the Holy Spirit, and even then, our unholy passions and desires seem to keep bubbling up to the surface and often need to be crucified daily until we have truly left all that baggage behind. Then we can travel free.

KEEP IN STEP WITH THE SPIRIT
Keeping in step with the Spirit means making decisions and choices based on the Holy Spirit's guidance: *'If we live by the Spirit, let us also keep in step with the Spirit'* (5.25).

The Galatians were shown by Barnabas, Paul and the team, how to live by the Spirit. If they did this, they could follow the right path and keep in step with the Spirit. Then they could live the victorious, spiritual life they have chosen.

As inheritors of those violent forebears who worked not so many years before as mercenaries, or had been mercenaries themselves, these Galatians knew about the need for marching soldiers to keep in step. If even one person got out of step the whole group was upset, and this was exactly what had happened to some of this band of new Christians. They had already chosen to go over to the other side to be soldiers of the Cross, but some had listened to the enticements and blandishments of new people with old ideas. It only took a few out of step to put the whole

Galatian church out of kilter. The harmony and unity of their forward progress had been shattered.

We, too, need to learn to keep in step with the Spirit and live holy, spiritual lives acceptable to God. Through our baptism we have died and been buried to sin and just as Christ was raised from the dead, so we are raised by the action of the Holy Spirit who gives us the power to live a new life in a new way, but we must utilize that power. To look at it another way, how foolish we would be to remain sitting in the dark when all we need to do is turn on the switch and use the power that is waiting for us to use.

To return to the metaphor of keeping in step, whether we are Celtic or not, we need to follow Jesus our leader into the battle against sin and the devil and keep in step without deviating. I am reminded here of the hymn, '*Onward Christian Soldiers.*' Thinking of mercenaries and soldiers also reminds me of the Salvation Army - and the Church Army, which is a branch of the Anglican/ Episcopal Church. It's no good if, as Christ's soldiers, we just march along in our lives blindly following the leader. We also need to keep alert and watch out for the enemy who might appear at any time and from any direction along the route.

GETTING OUT OF STEP IS DANGEROUS

Paul now referred to some more of the dangers that may have been bringing about problems in the Galatian churches and causing the people to get out of step with the Holy Spirit. With sure aim, Paul hits on some of these problems:
'Let us not become conceited, provoking one another, envying one another' (5.26).

Paul had discovered in their communication with him that in their new walk they were stumbling and falling into traps they had been unaware were hidden along the way.

1. **THE STUMBLING BLOCK OF CONCEIT**
   The Galatian converts were becoming conceited. Instead of looking outwards and to God, they had become proud of their status as Christians. With God on their side, they must be right; they could not possibly be wrong. They had become inward looking and were changing their focus from it being trained on their relationship with their Heavenly Father and were turning to think more of themselves. They were becoming self-centred.

   This attitude was leading them to unnecessarily provoke and goad each other. Because of the upset caused by the visiting preachers, undesirable facets of their traditional culture were coming to the surface and some of the people were deliberately setting out to make their fellow Christians annoyed and angry. When they had been following heathen religions, they had wallowed in dramatic differences and quarrels. This was not what Paul had wanted to hear about.

2. **THE STUMBLING BLOCK OF ENVY**
   At the same time some envied the advancement and achievements of the others. This was the thirteenth in Paul's list of 'works of the flesh.'[36] As we saw, the end result of this could even end in murder. If the Galatians were resorting to envy of one another, whether it was of their possessions or achievements in the Christian walk, it was something that Paul abhorred and sternly warned them against. We are not told how they were doing these things, but their problems were all connected because they were concentrating on thinking about themselves instead of assisting each other along the way. What should they have

---

[36] *See* p. 173

been doing? Keeping in step with the Holy Spirit, encouraging, serving and helping one another.

An interesting point in some of these words of Paul as he draws towards the close of his letter, is that he is again aligning himself with his Galatian brothers and sisters. Let us look at this passage again:

^{24}*And those who belong to Christ Jesus have crucified the flesh with its passions and desires.* ^{25}*If **we** live by the Spirit, let **us** also keep in step with the Spirit.* ^{26}*Let **us** not become conceited, provoking one another, envying one another.*

Paul confirmed that he counted himself as one who needs to keep in step, keep humble and fix his eyes on Jesus.

These traps are ways of the flesh and they can be danger signs for us, too, as we follow along the way. It's so easy to get out of step and stray from the path God has chosen for us. The Galatians, Celts today and, indeed, every Christian, must remain alert if we are to avoid these traps and pitfalls.

To Think About or Discuss

1. How well do we allow the Holy Spirit to guide our feet on our journey of life?

2. If you have read John Bunyan's Pilgrim's Progress, in what ways can you relate his tale to these words of Paul?

3. What is so dangerous about getting out of step with the Holy Spirit? How important is He on your life's journey?

≈28≈

THE NEW LIFE OF THE CHRISTIAN
CHAPTER 6. 1 - 6

6. *¹Brothers, if anyone is caught in any transgression, you who are spiritual should restore him in a spirit of gentleness. Keep watch on yourself, lest you too be tempted. ²Bear one another's burdens, and so fulfill the law of Christ. ³For if anyone thinks he is something, when he is nothing, he deceives himself. ⁴But let each one test his own work, and then his reason to boast will be in himself alone and not in his neighbor. ⁵For each will have to bear his own load. ⁶Let the one who is taught the word share all good things with the one who teaches.*

Paul reminded the Galatians that those who are spiritual have a responsibility towards other Christians, to help them when they err and fall, to bear each other's burdens as well as their own, to remain humble and to share together the way that God has worked in their lives. Although we may have obtained new life as Christians, we can still make mistakes. We can sin, forget to help others and may not remain humble or share with others.

ERRING BROTHERS AND SISTERS

It is easy to yield to temptation to do or think something we know is entering forbidden enemy territory. We like to think we are spiritual, mature Christians, but we are not immune. We experience temptation and err, and it is our duty and privilege to help our Christian brothers and sisters when they succumb to temptation. Paul tells us to '*restore such a one in a spirit of gentleness.*' Gentleness is one of the Fruits of the Spirit and we need to aid our brothers and sisters in a spirit of love and gentleness, being understanding, and non judgmental. This is the way for us to live a life of love in the Spirit.

BEAR ONE ANOTHER'S BURDENS
By writing to the Galatians, *'Bear one another's burdens'* (6.2a), Paul remined them to be thoughtful for each other, especially when life became difficult and burdensome for other members of the church. We, too, can serve by helping others, even by just being there and offering a listening ear. Followers of Christ gladly fulfill the will of their Saviour. When in a quandary, we can think about what He would do in a similar situation and even say aloud, 'What would Jesus do?' It can help in solving difficult problems.

WATCH OUR ACTIONS AND THOUGHTS
It's fine to be able to help others, but we are human and not perfect, so we should be alert and careful about our own behaviour. As Paul wrote, *'Keep watch on yourself, lest you too be tempted'* (6.2a). Even more mature Christians whose work is to minister to others must take care that they not transgress. It is easy to be led astray by our own desires or along non-Christian paths.

THE LAW OF CHRIST
Paul continued, *'and in this way you will fulfill the law of Christ'* (6.2b). The most important Law of all was Jesus' distillation of the Law of Moses, His command, firstly, to love God, and secondly, to love our neighbour as ourselves (Matthew 22.39, John 13.34), but do we obey it?

Jesus is our perfect model of how to live, and as Christians we should bear each other's burdens and so place ourselves under the Law of Christ. This is the Law that gives freedom and through it we are justified before God. The bearing of one another's burdens could never have occurred if they, or we, had remained under the burden of the Mosaic Law. It can only occur when we have the freedom to bear them through our faith in Jesus Christ.

BE HUMBLE

In the world, there is much talk about the importance of self-esteem, rather than being humble. This is different from seeing ourselves as God's loved and precious children; it is raising people's opinions of themselves so that they think they are better than others. It begins in the classroom and has become a very damaging educational concept. I started working life as a teacher and continue to be interested in what is happening in education. Some innovations are creative and exciting, but the current emphasis on self-esteem gives a child an unrealistic view of himself and his position in the world. However, fads come and go a little like a pendulum; once it has swung too far in one direction, it begins to swing the other way. Let's pray that it swings the other way soon so our children will be better prepared for life in the real world.

Paul reminded the Galatians that Christians are humble servants of God, *'For if those who are nothing think they are something, they deceive themselves'* (6.3). They should not deceive themselves by thinking they are important. Likewise, we should not deceive ourselves that we are important. Let us think for a moment about our motives. Why do we spend time studying the Word of God, offer to help in crèche at church, or give hospitality? I need to look at myself and ask, "What is my ultimate objective in doing these things? What will I do with my knowledge about God, once I have it?" If we pursue theological knowledge for its own sake, it will be bad for us; it will only succeed in making us proud and conceited. It is true there can be no spiritual health without doctrinal knowledge, but it is also true that we cannot be spiritually healthy if we seek knowledge for the wrong purpose. In a later letter, Paul warned (1 Corinthians 8.1-2) that *'Knowledge puffs up...If anyone imagines that he knows something, he does not yet know as he ought to know.''*

To concentrate on learning theological facts just for the sake of gaining knowledge will help no one. I remember the medieval work of an anonymous 1300s writer, '*The Cloud of Unknowing.*' He wrote that if we want to come closer to God in our meditation and to have true fellowship with Him, we need to 'unknow' our theological knowledge, become as God's children and concentrate on simplicity, meditating on simple words, such as God, Love, Praise. These are the things that count in growing our relationship with God.

BE ACCOUNTABLE

We should try and look objectively at what we do and assess what we have done in the light of Jesus' teaching, and not look askance at what our neighbour or fellow worker has done. We should take pride in what we do. As Paul wrote, '*let each one test his own work, and then his reason to boast will be in himself alone and not in his neighbour*' (Galatians 6.4).

That instruction was for the Celts so long ago, but it is just as valid for us. We should be able to stand back and look objectively at what we have done and know that we have worked to the very best of our ability. Here, Paul is writing about accountability and that is vital for each of us.

We each need to bear our own load (6.5) and be responsible for our own actions. Looking at this from another perspective, we all have burdens to bear, and we need to face that and acknowledge that these are our responsibility, and probably often of our own making, as well. We cannot simply pass those burdens onto someone else and expect them to pick up the pieces for us. However, there is One to whom we can turn and who will help us bear the load, our dear Saviour and Friend, Jesus Christ.

We have heard this before, but here it is refreshingly new. In the Old Testament we read, '*Cast your burden on the Lord'* (Psalm 55.22), and in the New Testament, '*We who are strong have an obligation to bear with the failings of the weak'* (Romans 15.1). Paul further develops this theme on our responsibility to help others in 1 Thessalonians 5.11: *'admonish the idle, encourage the faint-hearted, help the weak, be patient with them all.'*

As well as bearing our own burden, we should patiently waken the indolent to their responsibility, encourage others when they are flagging on the journey, and assist those who are weak and need extra strength. Finally, Paul reminds us to *'not be anxious: Casting all your anxiety on him because he cares for you'* (1 Peter 5.7).

ENCOURAGE THOSE WHO TEACH
Teaching and preaching are not easy, but Paul adds something else for those who are being taught: *'Let the one who is taught the word share in all good things with the one who teaches'* (Galatians 6.6). It is not only the time that is involved in teaching and preaching when the teacher or minister stands before the students or the congregation, but there are the hours of praying, reading and preparation that go into those lessons or sermons.

Paul exhorted the Galatians, as hearers of the Word, to encourage their teachers and to share their own experiences with them, especially encouraging them with good words of commendation and also sharing with them when something good happens. We, too, can share with our teachers and preachers when God answers our prayers, or when we make a break-through with someone we have been praying for and trying to help.

To Think About or Discuss

1. Discuss: As Paul is drawing closer to the end of his letter he seems to be changing to a more positive note. Why is this?

2. Paul referred to one of the Fruit of the Spirit and how it could be used when he wrote: *'you who are spiritual should restore him in a spirit of gentleness.'*
How can we do this?

3. List some of the good and bad reasons why we study the Scriptures.

4. Is there ever a good reason for boasting?
Did Paul ever boast about anything?

5. What are some of the ways in which we can *'share in all good things with the one who teaches?'*

≈29≈

THE NEW LIFE OF CARING
CHAPTER 6. 7 - 10

The new life in Jesus is to be a life of caring. Paul told the Galatians that they must learn to be careful about their own actions and thoughtful in the way that they cared for others.

6 ⁷Do not be deceived; God is not mocked, for whatever one sows, that he will also reap. ⁸For the one who sows to his own flesh, will from the flesh reap corruption, but the one who sows to the Spirit will from the Spirit reap eternal life. ⁹And let us not grow weary of doing good, for in due season we will reap, if we do not give up. ¹⁰So then, as we have opportunity, let us do good to everyone, and especially to those who are of the household of faith.

GOD IS ALL-SEEING
It's no good trying to pull the wool over God's eyes; He is All-seeing, *'Do not be deceived; God is not mocked'* (6.7a).

Paul told the Galatians that they should not allow these false teachers to deceive them and they should not deceive themselves either. God knew what had been said and taught to these Celts and He never allowed Himself to be mocked: those who tried to teach them in the wrong way were only deceiving themselves by being so certain that they were right. They could never deceive God.

SOWING AND REAPING
Paul warned that retribution would come: *'whatever one sows, that he will also reap'* (6.7b). In the end, God knew what the interlopers were attempting to do and ultimately they would bear the consequences of their misleading

message. They were responsible to God for their own words and actions.

We, too, need to be careful about what we do, think and say. In time it will catch up with us, sometimes sooner than later. This reminds me of a story I heard recently.

A mother took her little girl to visit her Grandfather who was ill in hospital. The little girl had been there before and ran ahead. She rushed into the room.

"Hullo, Grandpa," she greeted him excitedly, "As soon as Mummy comes in, would you please make a noise like a frog?"
"Why?" her Grandpa asked.
"Because I heard Mummy say that as soon as you croak, we can go to Disney World!"

Yes, we need to be careful what we say in front of the children, but we need to be even more careful about what we say and think before our Heavenly Father.

We can apply these words of Paul to ourselves: God does see everything we do and knows everything we think. If we say, 'There is no God,' and do and think whatever we wish, the time will come when there is a reckoning; God is not mocked and if we ignore Him and spend our lives sowing wild oats, that is what we will reap – a useless harvest to offer Him as our sacrifice on our last day.

SOWING TO THE FLESH
Paul then went back again in thought to what he had written before. *For the one who sows to his own flesh, will from the flesh reap corruption'* (6.8a).

Paul warned the Galatians that if they concentrated on the physical aspects and needs of their bodies, they would, in return, reap only corruption and dishonesty. It is the same for us. If we put ourselves first we become self-centred and the result will be that our lives are no longer Christ-centred. We must put Christ first.

Paul stressed the fact that if the Galatians surrendered themselves to their sinful desires that corruption would be embedded in their character and they would no longer be holy and acceptable as children of the Heavenly Father.

This statement in 6.8a can also be taken literally, with the same result: if the Galatians submitted to circumcision, they would then have to take on the Mosaic Law and this could only highlight their sinful nature and corrupt character.

SOW TO THE SPIRIT
Then Paul turned from the negative to the positive result, the harvest for those who retain their faith in Christ and sow to the Spirit: *'the one who sows to the Spirit will from the Spirit reap eternal life'* (6.8b).

For us, Paul's reference here to reaping looks forward to the blessing of eternal life that is bestowed on the believer as the culmination of his sowing his life to the Spirit. The reward, the harvest, will be 'out of this world!'

Paul had such knowledge of the Old Testament! I wonder if, in the back of his mind he was thinking here of some of the much-loved stories in the Scriptures? Could one of them have been the story of Esther and Mordecai? Through Mordecai's importunity, Esther saved his life, that of herself and the lives of thousands of other Jews living in Persia, yet in the whole of the little Book of Esther there is no mention of God. Granted, Mordecai was raised to a position second only to the king in a vast empire that stretched all the way to India.

The Jews were noble in that they took no plunder, but could it have been under God's guidance to order the slaughter of Haman's ten sons and the killing of thousands of Persians? Did He order the Jews to hold a feast to celebrate that massacre? Did He really decree that a two-day feast was to be held annually forever to celebrate this bloodbath of vengeance?

They were tough times and the despotic Persian King Ahasuerus did not bat an eyelid at the slaughter of a great number of his own subjects, both Persian and those of other nations, but this did not exempt the Jews from God's Law, 'Do not kill.' What did they reap, both on earth and in heaven?

PERSEVERE IN SERVING OTHERS
A little further back in this letter Paul reminded his Galatian readers of the importance of patience, one of the Fruit of the Spirit. We all know that waiting is not easy; we are, by nature, impatient. We know what we want and we want it yesterday. Yet Paul advises us to not grow weary in doing what is right, but to persevere:
'And let us not grow weary in doing good, for in due season we will reap, if we do not give up' (6.9).
The joyous harvest time will come.

While we believers await our rewards (6.7-9) we should make the most of every chance to do good for others, especially for other Christians, *'So then, as we have opportunity, let us do good to everyone, and especially to those of the household of faith'* (6.10).

Of course, here Paul was writing to the Galatians. He had a deep desire for them to look outward and upward, to look to Jesus and to learn to serve others, and especially to aim to serve their fellow Christians.

For us, too, as believers, whether we are Celtic or not, we should learn to rely on the strength and guidance of the Holy Spirit. We should not become weary on our 'journey,' but show and share that Fruit of the Spirit in the way we live our lives, taking every opportunity to help others in any way we can.

Earlier we discussed 'doing' the Law. As Paul drew near the end of his letter, he was impelled to emphasize the importance of Christians 'doing' good to others. How right that is as an aim for the Christian. In doing good, our primary focus should be on serving other believers, but not to the exclusion of people outside the church. They may be potential believers and can come closer to Christ through experiencing the love and goodness of Christian neighbours. This was really Paul's last word to his Celtic brothers and sisters in Christ.

To Think About or Discuss

1. How might we sow to our own flesh and what will the harvest be?

2. Paul wrote that *'the one who sows to the Spirit will from the Spirit reap eternal life.'*
   In what ways can we sow to the Spirit?

3. We know that we Christians are to do good and help others, but do we ever weary of this? We often hear of 'burn-out,' that people who have been serving so well suddenly become exhausted and give up. That is understandable, yet Paul exhorts the Galatians to continue. Why?

4. Discuss Paul's statement that we should do good *especially for other Christians*.

≈30≈

SUMMARY AND BENEDICTION
CHAPTER 6. 11 - 18

6 *[11]See with what large letters I am writing to you with my own hand! [12] It is those who want to make good showing in the flesh who would force you to be circumcised, and only in order that they may not be persecuted for the cross of Christ. [13] For even those who are circumcised do not themselves obey the law, but they desire to have you circumcised that they may boast in your flesh. [14]But far be it from me to boast except in the cross of our Lord Jesus Christ, by which the world has been crucified to me, and I to the world. [15]For neither circumcision counts for anything, nor uncircumcision, but a new creation. [16]And as for all who walk by this rule, peace and mercy be upon them, and upon the Israel of God.*
[17]From now on let no one cause me trouble, for I bear on my body the marks of Jesus.
[18]The grace of our Lord Jesus Christ be with your spirit, brothers. Amen.

This was Paul's PS, his postscript. In it he presented his concluding admonitions and a final reminder that for the Christian sacrificial living, in direct contrast to legalism, is the choice to make.

PAUL'S OWN HAND
Paul had probably been dictating his letter to a scribe, so he added, *[11] See with what large letters I am writing to you with my own hand!*

We can read about employing a scribe in his *Letter to the Romans* (Romans 16.22). It was the custom at that time, as, indeed it is today in the business world, to dictated a letter to a secretary. Now, he completes the letter in his own hand as he also did in his second letter to the Thessalonians (3.17).

FINAL WARNING
In his final warning, Paul summarized the main themes of his letter: *'It is those who want to make good showing in the flesh who would force you to be circumcised, and only in order that they may not be persecuted for the cross of Christ. For even those who are circumcised do not themselves obey the law, but they desire to have you circumcised that they may boast in your flesh'* (6.12-13).

In it he challenged the Galatians to stay true to the gospel. For a final time, he pointed out that if they complied with the demands of these false teachers and underwent circumcision, they would be denying the cross and turning their backs on the new creations that they had become through their faith in Jesus Christ.

Paul's main argument was that all legalistic versions of the Gospel are perversions of it. We can see that this is just as pertinent today for all Celts and everyone else. Our enjoyment of Christian freedom and liberty depends solely on our salvation by God's grace alone, through Christ alone, and received by faith alone.

NEW LIFE AND THE CROSS
As a Jew, Paul had learned the Mosaic Law well and could boast of his proficiency and knowledge of it. Now he has reiterated that while Jews can boast of their knowledge of the Law, they cannot keep it; they transgress and are unable to completely 'do' the Law. He can never boast of how this can achieve righteousness in God's sight, *'But far be it from me to boast except in the cross of our Lord Jesus Christ, by which the world has been crucified to me, and I to the world'* (6.14).

Ever since Paul had met Christ on the road to Damascus, the world has been crucified to him. This is the only thing in the whole universe that he can possibly boast about.

The Galatian Christians could choose to learn the Law and try to keep it and obey it, but they could never live the Law. Christ now lived in Paul and He lived in Christ. The world no longer attracted and influenced Paul. This was his hope for these Celts and it is our hope and prayer for all who puts their faith in Christ Jesus.

A NEW CREATION IN CHRIST

Paul again emphasized that since Christ was sacrificed on the cross for our sins, these outward signs are irrelevant; they are nothing, *'For neither circumcision counts for anything, nor uncircumcision, but a new creation'* (6.15).

Such signs belong to the old precepts of the Law; the only thing that counts is to become a new creation.

In a number of his later letters Paul continued this negative attitude towards keeping the Commandments that God gave to Moses; they are no longer to be considered, the Law has been fulfilled by Jesus and is now obsolete; it is nothing, null and void for the believer. As we saw in verse 14, the whole world had changed. There is still a new world to come, but we're definitely on the way. The new creation is not just within ourselves, but it is the whole of the world as well. That is to be the new creation.

Jesus is the New Covenant and as Paul wrote later, the Old Covenant had been superseded. This is what had been promised by so many of the prophets in the Old Testament Scriptures over hundreds of years. The prophecy had come to pass. God had kept His promise and sent the Messiah. Now the old Law had passed away and through the death and resurrection of Jesus everything had been made new.

When we accept that gift through the grace of God we ourselves are a 'new creation' and that is all that we need as Christians. It is everything! Whatever else is required will follow. The Law has been fulfilled. That is positivity.

Paul wrote more on this theme in later letters, such as in 2 Corinthians 5.1. As believers we are new creatures and part of the new creation of the world that is to come. The new world began with Christ and we are part of that gradual creation process. God's timing is perfect. We can read more about this in The Revelation to John, but that had not yet been written when Paul wrote this letter.

A NEW LIFE OF PEACE

If the Galatians followed this one simple, but profound rule, and Paul was confident that they would do so after receiving his letter, then he blessed them with 'peace and mercy.' God, too, will bless them: *'And as for all who walk by this rule, peace and mercy be upon them, and upon the Israel of God'* (6.14).

Here Paul was contrasting the 'present Jerusalem' that he wrote of in 4.26, with the Israel of God. The true people of God are the believing descendants of Abraham.[37] They belong to the 'Jerusalem above' (4.26-27). That promise is not only for the Galatians, but also for all Christians through the ages and it still stands for us today.

The false teachers and perhaps some of the Galatian Christians, too, had been misrepresenting Paul and he desired that they would understand the sincerity of his message; he wanted no more trouble of this kind: *'From now on let no one cause me trouble, for I bear on my body the marks of Jesus'* (6.17). He insisted on the respect that was due to his ministry and calling as one of the special group of Apostles. He was a genuine servant of Christ and

---

[37] *see* Galatians 3.7 and 29

had the physical scars to prove it. Here he was referring to the results of his being persecuted, scars from when he was lashed and stoned; these he called the 'marks of Jesus' (*see* 2 Cor. 11.23-27).

CLOSING BENEDICTION

Paul's final prayerful blessing was: '*The grace of our Lord Jesus Christ be with your spirit, brothers. Amen*' (6.18).

This blessing clearly showed the Galatians that he had not given up on them. He continued to refer to them as brothers and sisters and called on Christ and the Holy Spirit to give them grace.

This blessing remains for us as Christian brothers and sisters, today. Praise God that He never gives up on us! The grace of our Lord Jesus Christ is with us.

To Think About or Discuss

1. What do you see as the main themes of Paul's letter?
   For the Galatians? Are they the same for us today?

2. We often use the word 'sophisticated,' thinking that it describes a person as being cultured and that it is something to admire. We wish that we could change to be a new creation like that. How would Paul look at the word in the light of the fact that it can also mean worldly-wise and artificial?

3. What do you know from other sources in the New Testament about the marks of Jesus on Paul's body?

4. Do we ever wish our Christian brothers and sisters peace and mercy and the grace of our Lord Jesus Christ?
   We may want to use a blessing like this and to receive a blessing like this, too.
   How can this be done in the context of our current day and age?

≈31≈

CONCLUDING REMARKS

It has been an interesting journey together as we have studied Paul's *Letter to the Galatians* and, as fellow Christians, I have learned much from it and I hope that you have, too.

As we have seen, Paul understood these new Galatian Christians very well and we can see this understanding throughout this, his first preserved letter, and probably especially in his list of their failings. These can so easily be our failings, too. He listed fifteen of them to add to these Celts' propensity to welcome and listen to false teachers. However, he offset against these all the good qualities they could aim for – nine of them. None of these failings, or of the achievable good qualities, the Fruit of the Spirit, which figured so prominently in his letter, is specifically named in the Ten Commandments, the basis of all the Law of the Old Testament. Paul knew that these people were capable of overcoming their failings and of growing these Fruit of the Spirit in their lives with the loving grace of the Father, faith in Jesus Christ, and the power and guidance of the Holy Spirit.

We have looked at Paul's letter in some detail and examined his logical, well thought out arguments and his stories and examples that supported and defended his reasoning. These help us to understand further what this brilliant young man was writing to these wavering Celts whose concern he had taken so much to heart. It had not been the intention of the missionary group to take their message to these fiery pagans, but due to his physical ailment that caused their enforced stay, and the guidance of the Holy Spirit, he had learned to love them and to be very concerned for their spiritual wellbeing.

When my husband and I were in missionary training college, one thing we were told by a dear old returned missionary stuck like a burr in our minds: it was that our first placement would always remain dear in our hearts. We found this to be true, although it does not mean we loved the people in later assignments any less. This must have been Paul's experience, too. The spiritual health and growth of these Galatians weighed heavily on his heart and he really felt personally responsible when they were led astray. He had worked, prayed for them, led them to Christ, and built lovely relationships with a volatile people who had previously only known heathen ways.

Through Paul's teaching and the guidance of the Holy Spirit, the Galatians had made the decision to follow Christ and had now become Christians, so for them the Law was no longer relevant, but even the most holy of Christians is not perfect.

These new converts were yet babes in Christ and because of their Celtic cultural heritage they could be very strong when things were going their way, but when difficulties arose, they were prone to lose their way and then confusion reigned. They needed to learn to rely on God, to trust Him for everything, to listen to Him in their hearts and acquire discernment. They needed to learn how to stand back and look at problems objectively in His strength and peace, so they might be enabled to examine obstacles thoughtfully and logically in the light of the knowledge they had already gained. To rush off on a tangent when they were pressured to embrace new, enticing alternatives was not God's plan for them. By learning to stand fast they could retain God's peace in their hearts and come to rely on Him, their Father, and trust Him for everything in their lives.

That was Paul's message and prayer for these Galatian Celts. It is the way for all of us to move towards maturity as Christians.

How wonderful it is that through Jesus Christ the Law that God gave His people through Moses has been fulfilled! The ancient promise, the Covenant between Abraham and God, still stands. Through putting our faith in the promised offspring, the Lord Jesus Christ, the blessings of God can now be poured out on all, both Gentile and Jew. All that is needed is faith in Jesus.

Not only those who are Celts, but every individual person can apply Paul's words in their own life and learn so much from this *Letter of Paul to the Galatians* in our life's journey even today, almost two thousand years later.

Let us praise our Triune God for Paul and his great insights in his letters that have been preserved for so long and have come down the ages to continue to speak to each of us personally today.

We, His children, say a humble, "Thank you, Father."

APPENDIX 1

A BRIEF TIMELINE OF THE GALATIAN CELTS

Much has been written about the history of the Celts and those they came into contact and conflict with, but the information and dates often seem to be in conflict, too. The following has been gleaned from a wide variety of sources and information already known by the author.

500s B.C. – 100 B.C.
During these years the warlike tribes of Gauls were moving and extending in several directions. They were the ruling power of barbarian Europe. In Paul's letter to the Galatians we have a portrait of the traditional notion of the Celt in those times.

400s Etruria was a country in what is now modern Tuscany in northern Italy. One of the towns founded by the Etruscans in about 524 BC was Bologna. Gauls had occupied an area just north of Etruria and there was often fighting along the border. A funerary *stela*, or grave-marker that was found in Bologna shows a naked Celtic foot soldier in conflict with a mounted Etruscan. It was quite common in the Celtic world to fight naked. The Etruscan civilization was very ancient and Etruria did not become a Roman colony until 189 BC.

400 The Gauls advanced southward and came into dangerous conflict with Rome.

300s B.C.
Hordes of Celtic warriors who were sometimes accompanied by their migrating communities,

thrust southward into Italy, Greece and Asia Minor. The Celtic stereotype was described as a wild, fearless warrior who was irrationally brave in the first onslaught, but who was prone to wild despair when the battle turned against him.

390   The Gauls reached the Greek world.

369   Celtic warriors were employed as mercenary troops in a war between Sparta and Thebes, cities in ancient Greece. Later, thanks to the Theban leader, Epameinondas, they won.

Plato (c429-347 BC), the Greek philosopher, described the Celts as warlike and hard drinking 'barbarians.'

Aristotle (384-322) wrote that the Celts were hardy northerners who exposed their children, with little clothing on them, to the harsh climate in order to toughen them; he also wrote that excessive obesity among Celtic men was punished. He described the men as warlike, ferocious and fearless to the point of irrationality.

According to Aristotle, the men took little notice of their women, preferring male company. They had strict rules of hospitality, especially to strangers. He also wrote about Druids and holy men among the Celts and Galatae.

Greek Mythology: The Celts even featured in Greek mythology. According to this, the Celts were descended from a union of Polyphemus and either Galatea or the giant Keltos, descendants of Galatos, son of Cyclops. Galatea's father was Heracles who came from Thebes.

361   The Roman, Manlius, fought a Celtic chieftain in single combat. It was noted again that the Celt fought naked except for his shield, two swords, a torc and armlets. The torc was a circle of woven strands of metal twisted together; it opened at the front and was worn around the neck as a symbol of strength and power.

200s B.C.

The barbarian Celts were again on the move. The acropolis of Pergamum in Western Turkey was the focus of Pergamene power. There were two important religious precincts, the temple of Athena and the altar of Zeus. Both had sculptures celebrating Pergamene victories for saving Greece from the Celtic raiders. Throughout the century, after their initial migration from Europe, the Gauls continued to confront both the Hellenistic and Roman armies.

280-278 This was a time of Celtic invasion of Greece, including an attack on Delphi and the first incursion of Celts into Asia Minor with new bands arriving from time to time from Europe.

279   This date is remembered as the beginning of great Gallic inroads in several directions. Three tribes of raiders entered Anatolia from the Danube region. 'Gaul' was the name used by the Roman historian Livy.

The Celts maintained their distinctive lifestyle with raids and mercenary activity being an essential part of their social system. As time went on, large Roman estates increased and became better defended. When the Celts were beaten they contributed to the slave labour needed on these estates; they also drifted from the farms to the cities.

278-7 King Nicomedes of Bithynia invited the Gauls to serve as mercenaries in his conflicts with his neighbour, Antiochus 1. Twenty thousand Celts arrived. They had been separated from the main force that attacked Delphi. They crossed the water between Europe and Asia and moved into Asia Minor where they collectively became known as Galatians. There were two separate tribes under the leadership of Leonorios and Lutorius. They were in search of new land to settle and half of the migrants were non-fighters: the women, children and the aged. King Nicomedes settled them in the disputed territory between his own kingdom of Bithynia and that ruled by Antiochus.

Later the Celts moved to the barren highland area east of Ankara that flanked the Halys, the longest river in Turkey. Although the Galatians kept their traditions and customs, they adopted indigenous styles and technologies when they built their forts.

275-4 A period of instability followed. It culminated in the defeat of the Celts by the Seleucid king, Antiochus 1 in the famous 'Elephant Battle.' The Gauls had never seen elephants before and Antiochus' troop included sixteen elephants that terrified them so much that those who were not trampled to death fled.

By this time there were three tribal groups that all spoke the same language: the Tolistobogii, the Trocmi and the Tectosages. Each group laid claim to a territory to rampage and raid, while they also providing mercenary services for any Hellenistic potentate who required their assistance. It was a mobile phase of their occupation.

263-241　The Celtic raids in Asia Minor began to escalate: Eumens 1 of Pergamom, the prime power in the west, decided to pay them tribute to keep them quieter.

In the latter part of the 200s BC, the Celts were used extensively as mercenaries in the armies of both the Seleucid and Ptolemaic (Egyptian) rulers. However, they continued to become increasingly unruly and unreliable. The Seleucid rulers were part of a Macedonian dynastic empire in Asia Minor, covering Syria, Persia, Bactria and Babylonia.

At one stage a Celtic group became so demoralized by the eclipse of the moon they decided to change to fighting for the opposite side, so they and their families were sent to Hellespont, the narrow passage between the Aegean Sea and the Sea of Marmara, which today is the Dardanelles in Turkey.

241　The Celts continued to be a problem until 197 BC, and they maintained a high degree of mobility as their raids intensified. Attelus 1, the ruler who followed Eumens 1 of Pergamom, decided to stand his ground.

233　Attelus 1 won a decisive battle at the Springs of Kailos. To celebrate, a Greek statue of 'The Dying Galatian,' thought to have been in bronze was erected on the acropolis of Pergamum on Turkey's Aegean coast. It was lost, but some copies were made and the most famous to survive is a Roman marble one, sometimes known as 'The Dying Gaul.'

232　Due to this major defeat, the Celts were compelled to concentrate in Phrygia. An agreement was made with Attelus1 to cease raiding the Pergamene kingdom, although he permitted some territorial expansion east of the river Halys. This agreement marks the point at which Galatia became a recognized territory.

By now the indigenous population of Phrygia had been absorbed and the Celts must have become ethnically mixed to some extent. However, the social structure remained little changed. Each of the three tribes was divided into four parts, or tetrarchies, and each had its own tetrarch, a judge, a war leader, and two subordinate commanders who answered to him. A Council that represented the twelve tetrarchies was made up of three hundred men.

The Council met at Drunemeton, a sacred place of the Iron Age. For the Galatians in Asia Minor it was connected with the Druids, Nemeton meaning 'sacred enclosure.' The duties of the tetrarchies included passing judgment on murder cases and a separation of leadership between civil and military leadership and the distinct judicial class. They met once a year under Druidic authority. There was a strong religious focus and the Druids were the controlling religious authority.

229 Until about 229 BC, the Celts were a scourge to the surrounding cities. They made frequent raids from their home base, especially against the rich Hellenized cities.

227 The Celts remained mobile within a large area; one group reached Gallipoli, but was then defeated by Antigonos II.

225 In the Battle of Telamon, according to the Greek historian, Polybius, the Celtic Gaesatae (spear

men) warriors still fought naked except for the sword belt and their rich adornments of gold neck torcs and armlets. The finely built men had terrifying appearances and gestures. The Roman philosopher, Plybius, wrote that he thought they discarded their clothes because they were a hindrance in battle, but it is now thought that it may have had some ritual significance.

Certainly the torc had deep religious significance; deities are shown as wearing torcs and it was believed that they gave the wearer a sense of being protected by the gods, also that they were a symbol of the wearer's life and being.

218 Attelus II employed Gallic Aigosage mercenaries in campaigns in both Aeolis and Phrygia. Later he gave them lands on the borders of Phrygia. Once they were settled the Celts began making extensive raids until Prusias of Bithynia wiped out the entire Celtic population.

213-12 In Thrace, Celtic power lasted for two generations longer before their influence was destroyed.

100s B.C.

After this other Celtic groups received many defeats.

191 A Roman army defeated the Celts at Bologna, Italy. The spoils included one thousand, five hundred gold torcs.

190 The Seleucid army and its Galatian mercenaries were soundly defeated in a clash between a combined Roman and Pergamene force.

189 A Roman Centurion, Manlius Vulso, set out for central Anatolia, the Galatian's home territory.

The Tolistobogii and Trocmi fighting men rallied at Mount Olympus, near Pessinus. The Tectosages and families of the Trocmi went to Mount Magaba.

After nearly a century of experience in Asia Minor, the pattern had not changed: the stereotype of the Celt as a fighting man was the Galatian still using the archaic type of Celtic shield and fighting naked. It was noted that their bodies were plump and white, as they were never exposed except in battle. Manlius first defeated the Tolistobogii and then the Trocmi. The wounds of the white bodied Celts showed vividly as the Romans cut them to pieces. Manlius took forty thousand men, women and children and sold them as slaves. Then he defeated the Tectosages.

The Galatians who were left agreed to stop all raids in western Asia Minor. The Roman commander described the Gauls as a degenerate, mixed race, referring to them as Gallogrecians. In his report there was no mention of towns, although the Trocmi had three walled garrisons: Danala, Tithridatium, and one at Tavium that was also the local emporium.

The Tetosages had a fortress at Ancyra while the Tolitobogii had fortresses at Blucium and Peium. Blucium was the royal residence of King Deiotarus, the chief Tetrach of the Tolistobogii, and his treasure was stored at Peium. He remained king of all Galatia until his death in 140 BC. Galatian society preferred to live in rural areas with fortified enclosures and a few trading centres; one was at a major shrine. They had left the Phrygian towns to decay.

Ortagion, a Tolistobogii chieftain tried to unite the Galatians under his headship to make war on

Pergamum, but he was unsuccessful. The Galatians also fought fierce battles among themselves. Ortagion's wife, Chiomora was captured by the Romans and raped by a centurion. The Romans ensured that the Galatians remained free from Pergamene control and a type of peace prevailed, however, the Galatian state remained independent and isolated.

167   The Galatian raids and attacks restarted. Eumenes II undertook vigorous campaigns to stop them.

165   The Pergamenes were successful and a new peace treaty was made. To celebrate their victory, the Pergamenes added a frieze to the altar of Zeus, and on the Athenian acropolis a monument was dedicated. Like the Greeks they were seen as saviours of the civilized world.

The Celts continued their barbarous practices, which included the belief that they needed to sacrifice the best of the spoils of war to the deities. The most important prisoners they took were sacrificed to the gods and the less important were speared.

123   By this time, the Celts were once again a power in the region.

100 – 0 B.C.

100   There were many Gallic slaves in Italy working on the large estates that were producing corn, oil and wine. It was estimated that there were three hundred thousand Celtic slaves there and that the number was increasing at the rate of fifteen thousand a year.

89	In Galatia, the system of tetrarchs was still in force.
88	Raids were needed for the maintenance of Celtic society. They raided Cappadocia and later Pontus. Mithridates IV of Pontus had been fighting the Romans and he now had this problem as well. He invited the Galatian chiefs to meet him at Pergamum. Hospitality was very important to the Galatians and sixty of the chiefs attended. All, but one, were massacred; those who did not attend were also killed and only three escaped. This considerably weakened the ruling Galatian elite.
	The Celts' leadership was divided and inefficient in dealing with problems of their rapidly changing world. The incident drove the Galatians over to the Roman side and the Romans encouraged a more unified leadership. Although they became pro-Roman and absorbed some of their ways, they remained independent and comparatively isolated.
67	Pompey, the Roman military leader, and a contemporary of Caesar annexed the Galatians' territory. It appears that there is little evidence of a change in their culture and that the allegiance was purely political.
25	Although Galatia had been annexed by Rome, Ancyra, Pessinus and Tavium remained the capitals of the three tribes.

50 – 300s A.D.

50s A.D.

By the time that Paul wrote his letter to the Galatians, there appear to have been few differences between Galatia and any other community in the Roman world although, even as a minority group they continued to maintain a high degree of ethnic identity. The Galatian cities were using Hellenistic building techniques but the fortified sites remained as typical Celtic hill forts.

60   In Britain, when the Celtic Queen, Boadicea, led troops into battle, she wore a cloak and gold torc and carried a spear.

100s A.D.

Allegiance continued to develop between the Galatian leaders and Roman authorities, but it was still only a political relationship and the Galatian communities seem to have retained much of their culture, including their social structure.

The Galatians also retained their sense of ethnic identity, and this reflects the deep-rooted strength of their Celtic tradition. Their language also continued to persist, although it is probable that they also read and spoke the local Greek as it is thought that this was the language Paul used in his letter.

300s A.D.

St Jerome, who lived at the end of the 4th century AD, wrote in a commentary on Galatians, that the language spoken by the Galatians of Asia Minor was similar to what he had heard spoken among the Treveri at Trier, where he had stayed; both peoples had Celtic ancestry.

APPENDIX 2

GALATIAN LANGUAGE

The 'barbarian' Celts hail from at least the Iron Age, and for much of the long passage of history they had no written record of their own. By the time that Paul wrote his *Letter to the Galatians* they kept his letter, so it must have been considered very special and precious for them. Presumably, as time had gone on, the Greek and Roman influences meant that they had learned to read and write, otherwise Paul would not have written to them.

Continental Celtic is the modern generic name for the languages spoken by the people known to classical writers, in the Greek as Keltoi or Keltai, especially for those on the Iberian Peninsula and southwest Germany, and in Latin as Celtae and the Galatae. Names at various times were changed according to the name of the particular tribe that was referred to during a period of about a thousand years, from 500 BC to 500 AD. These Celts occupied an area that stretched from Gaul to Iberia in the south, and Galatia in the east.

By 500 BC, Continental Celts were living in north-northeast France, southwest Germany, and Bohemia. It has been established by a number of writers that the Galatians were part of the Belgae Celts and the language of the Belgae was a Brythonic dialect, known as Gaulish.

After seven hundred years of living in a country where the common language was Greek, the Galatians had retained their language so well that it could be understood by linguistic kinsfolk living in other areas.

APPENDIX 3

GALATIAN RELIGION

As shown under the year 232 BC in Appendix 1, the Celts were a very religious people and the religious leaders of the tribes were known as Druids. As time went on, the Celts assimilated indigenous cults of the areas where they settled and so also worshipped a variety of local gods as well as their own.

As one example, Pesinus, a city in Anatolia on the Sakary River was a town in Phrygia. This city of Pesinus was famous for the cult of Cybele, a Phrygian goddess.

However, this cult spread to both Greece and Rome. Interestingly, the high priest during the time of Paul's visit was a Celt and half the college of priests at the temple was of Celtic birth. Worship of Cybele had spread to ancient Greece and the temple was seen as an especially holy place. The Pergamene kings had built it up and refurbished it, and it was impressive: the sanctuary and porticoes were made of white marble and it was seen as a thoroughly Hellenized place.

Cybele was the goddess of caverns, and of earth in its primitive state. She was worshipped on the top of mountains. For the Romans, she was the mother of the gods and the worship of this goddess was often wild, emotional, bloody and orgiastic, which probably appealed to the Galatians.

The Galatians also retained worship of their own deities as well (*see* Appendices 1 and 4).

APPENDIX 4

GALATIAN CULTURE

The Celtic society was strongly hierarchic. A number of writers, both before Christ and afterwards, made numerous generalizations that were the result of their contact with the Galatians. These included Caesar, who thought that there was a simple basic structure behind the social system of Celtic communities and that there were only two classes of significance, the Druids and the knights. He saw the rest as similar to slaves.

Some of Caesar's comments are interesting. He wrote that the knights were constantly involved in warfare and that some commanded huge entourages. As an example, he cited the Helvetian Orgetorix household: it consisted of ten thousand, and while this excluded dependents and debtors, it did include semi free medieval bondmen.

We learn more from the writing of a Greek philosopher named Poseidonius who was born about 135 B.C. in the Helenistic city of Apameia in Northern Syria. He held political office in Rhodes and travelled through much of the Roman world, including Greece, Italy and Gaul, and served as ambassador to Rome 87-86 B.C.

During his travels, Poseidonius studied the Celts and left vivid descriptions of what he saw. He noted that the Celtic social classes were carefully distinguished and their laws gave rigidity to the class system. Evidently the men's appearances were what distinguished between the classes; he described the nobles as having shaved cheeks but they let their moustaches grow freely to cover their mouths, while the Celtic elite shaved entirely or grew short beards.

Poseidonius also remarked on the skulls he saw that were nailed above Celtic doorways as trophies of war. He believed that the Druids were philosophers in whom 'pride and passion give way to wisdom,' that they were particularly honoured by the Celts, and that the Celts worshipped the Muses.

Other travellers made observations, too. One was that when the Gauls received gifts, they redistributed them to friends and relatives; that there was a competitive atmosphere among them, that they loved to feast, and they consumed alcohol rather liberally. It was found that their belief in an afterlife meant that they were willing to die in the interest of renown.

Hospitality was a very important part of Celtic culture. They offered hospitality to strangers, and needed to offer food and drink before finding out a visitor's business. On more than one occasion, their rigorous rules that covered hospitality were manipulated by the Romans. They were bound by custom and tradition to a system that involved trust, and opponents often abused this for own advantage.